the
powered
by protein
cookbook

The **POWERED BY PROTEIN**

Cookbook

Simple, Delicious,
High—Protein Recipes

Jackie Hartlaub

PHOTOGRAPHS BY MATT ARMENDARIZ

Clarkson Potter/Publishers
New York

contents

introduction

If you're reading this, there's a pretty good chance you're here because you've seen my protein-forward cooking videos online, where I used to post as @lowcarbstateofmind. (I've since changed my handle—more on that later!) I'm so honored that millions of people have turned to my videos as a way to help them take control of what fuels them, and to have a delicious time doing it.

Growing up, some of my favorite memories were going out to eat with my grandma, watching just about anything that aired on Food Network, and making (extremely silly) YouTube videos with my little brother and childhood friends. So looking back now, it's no surprise I ended up doing what I do today—creating cooking videos. My first job when I was in high school was a delivery driver position at a small, family-owned place called Adamo's Pizza. It had a tiny kitchen, but a kitchen nonetheless, and that was the start of my journey with cooking.

In college, I was always the one cooking for my roommates and friends. I will never forget the first steak I ever cooked in my first apartment, my sophomore year of college. My mom sent me back to school with a pack of Omaha steaks—to cook them, I remember she recommended I broil them in the oven, from start to finish. Surprisingly, they turned out great. I also remember the time I attempted to make guacamole in a Magic Bullet after a night out . . . let's just say, as much as I love shortcuts—you'll see lots of them in this book—that was a shortcut I never took again! After college, a group of my friends hosted dinner parties almost every weekend, and that's when I began to realize how much I really loved cooking. I was thirsty to learn how to cook all of my favorite dishes.

Fast forward five years later—now, I create recipe videos online and have a weekly newsletter. I am so grateful to have such a large community that loves and enjoys my recipes, whether they cook them word-for-word or just take inspiration from them to create simple, easy, protein-forward dinners. This book is a collection of mostly all-new recipes that I'm so excited to share with you, as well as some existing ones that have gotten so much attention online that I wanted to put them all in one place for you—like my Greek Salad with Chicken (page 82), Sesame-Crusted Tuna with

Soy-Ginger Sauce (page 162), BBQ "Chicken Crust" Pizza (page 89), and so many more.

Before I started creating content online, I struggled quite a bit with my own health, which is actually what led me to start sharing my recipes in the first place. I had always struggled with my weight growing up, but as I got older, my overall health started to scare me. Like a ton of people, I gained the "freshman 15" when I went to college, but for me, it ended up being more like the "freshman 30," and it sadly didn't stop when I came home. I honestly thought it was kind of a normal thing for people to deal with the symptoms I was dealing with. I was in my early 20s, I didn't have a regular menstrual cycle, I had heartburn constantly, and had absolutely zero confidence in myself.

My health journey truly began with the keto diet. I was an Ironworker for Local 63 in Chicago, and my work partner at the time said something to me that really hit home. I had just joined this fairly big company, and I was still very green. As a more experienced journeyman, he was giving some advice: "To do well in this industry, you really have to be healthy."

Sometimes, you already know something deep down, but it takes hearing it from someone else for it to really click. Jim's words were a big realization moment for me, and I decided I was going to learn how to take better care of myself—not only for myself, but because I genuinely wanted to do well in my career! A close friend had just started following a strict keto diet and lost about 30 pounds, so I decided to quietly try it myself. I didn't tell anyone, just in case I gave up or didn't see results, but keto actually worked pretty well for me, for a while—I lost around 60 pounds. Losing the weight was great, but to be honest, the best part was all the other feelings of well-being that came with it. For the first time in a long time, I completely stopped getting heartburn, my cycle slowly began to regulate, and I was actually feeling confident and motivated in my life. It may sound silly to some, but before I started the keto diet, I struggled to take care of myself. Just doing things day to day was not always easy for me, especially my job, which was quite labor-intensive. Like many people who start a health journey and lose some weight, I started feeling more confidence, which is not something I had a lot of before, and overall, I was a lot happier. Around that time, I began making videos of my keto recipes online, which is how most of my audience first found me in 2020.

While the keto diet was clearly helpful for me, looking back now it was really just a stepping stone for me with learning more about my health and how to better take care of myself. After a while, I realized that cutting out an entire food group—carbs—wasn't sustainable for me long-term. Which I unfortunately learned the hard way, maybe so you don't have to! I found myself overeating carbs whenever I did have them, and that's why I no longer recommend being super restrictive and why I ended up changing my social media handles from @lowcarbstateofmind to my full name instead. Over time, I found that a more balanced approach with carbs—more so just mindful about not overeating them—was crucial to finding a healthy balance for me in my diet. And that's key to this, too—I believe our diets shouldn't feel so complicated or restrictive at the end of the day. Getting rid of the "all or none" mentality around carbs and sugar helped me so much, and I think everyone has to find a way of eating that is sustainable—and enjoyable—to them.

Now, my meals are less about what I avoid and more about what I prioritize, specifically protein. Learning how to get around 30 grams of protein at each meal has been a game-changer for me. Every day I strive for at least 100 grams of protein (I aim for 1 gram per pound of my ideal body weight). Protein keeps you feeling full, especially important when eating with a calorie deficit, and helps you keep muscle mass while losing body fat. That's why I created this book—to share easy, protein-forward recipes that make meeting your protein goals easy, accessible, and yummy.

If I am being honest, I don't follow a specific diet anymore, and I intentionally try not to. Beyond protein intake, I've learned there are many factors that play a role in wellness and weight management for me. While I've maintained my weight loss from the keto diet for nearly five years—and even lost an additional 20 pounds—I've found certain habits are essential for me besides focusing on protein. These are the practices, mostly outside of food, that have made a huge difference for me and I think are worth mentioning, though you should trust your own doctor, nutritionist, and most of all your own body first to figure out what works for you.

* I no longer fast in the morning, and I eat breakfast within an hour of waking up.

* I wait to drink coffee until after breakfast (roughly 90 minutes after waking up) to help lower cortisol levels and avoid an afternoon crash.

* I prioritize getting daily morning sunlight (5 to 10 minutes outside) to help regulate my circadian rhythm and melatonin production for quality sleep.

* I wake up and go to bed at the same time every day to help regulate my circadian rhythm.

* I aim for 7 to 9 hours of quality sleep per night.

* I eat meals around the same time every day to balance blood sugar.

* I avoid too many fried foods, specifically anything fried in seed oils.

* I moderate my diet to have a lower overall carb intake, typically 70 to 90 grams per day.

I know some of the things on this list may not be what you'd expect to see in a cookbook, but there's a reason I include them. They're a crash course on the most important things I've learned about balancing my blood sugar and my circadian rhythm over the past five years, and they have made a huge difference for me.

If you're unfamiliar with circadian rhythm, it's just your body's natural 24-hour clock. It's the system of the body that helps regulate sleep-and-wake cycles and overall energy levels, based on light and dark cues throughout the day. Keeping your circadian rhythm regulated can help your overall health, energy, and mood. When it comes to building healthy habits, especially if you're working toward weight loss, experiencing a calorie deficit without a balanced circadian rhythm can feel like an uphill battle, especially in today's fast-paced world. To me, these rhythms and routines are just about as essential as the food itself.

Although I don't eat a strict keto diet anymore, carbohydrates are still something that I focus on because it's really easy to overeat them, and too many carbohydrates (or too much sugar) will mess with your insulin and blood sugar. So I would say I am very mindful about the overall amount of carbs I eat, and I make sure I combine carbs with fats and protein to avoid a blood sugar spike. I also like to use a technique I learned from Jessie Inchauspé, the Glucose Goddess (@glucosegoddess), which is to eat in a strategic order. Starting a meal with fiber from vegetables, then eating the protein, and then ending with carbs is really helpful when it comes to avoiding huge blood sugar spikes.

I know this is supposed to be just a cookbook, but for me, food and health are deeply connected. It would feel like I was leaving out a huge piece of the puzzle if I didn't also share with you guys the habits that allow me to make the best choices for myself every day—and to maintain the weight I have lost over the years.

But back to the recipes—probably the main reason you picked up this book! I'll be honest: This book isn't for those seeking upscale, Michelin-star meals. It's made for the busy—and sometimes lazy—home cook who wants easy, comforting meals that are protein-packed. Each recipe is designed to help you meet your daily protein goals while still truly enjoying what you eat.

Inside, you'll find tons of favorites to add to your cooking rotation, like my Louisiana Hot Honey Air-Fryer Chicken Thighs (page 61), Smoky Air-Fryer Old Bay–Mustard Salmon (page 157), Sheet-Pan Fajitas with Green Chile Crema (page 78), and more. I've also included some new favorites of mine, like Chuck Roast Chili (page 119), Spicy Jumbo Italian Meatballs (page 134), Air-Fryer Pork Chops (page 221), and more.

I hope you find my recipes are comforting, nourishing, and flavorful, giving you access to dishes that satisfy and fit easily into a busy lifestyle. Whether you're cooking for family, friends, or just yourself, there's something here for every craving. So, let's get cooking!

A note on nutritional analysis:

If you're tracking macros, I wanted to make these recipes easy for you to use. I worked with Abby Gerstein of Nutritional Solutions to analyze the amount of calories, protein, carbs, and fat in each recipe. Here are some things for you to keep in mind:

* When a recipe gives a choice of ingredients, the first choice is the one used in the analysis.

* When a range of ingredient amounts is given, the smaller amount is used.

* Optional or "for serving" ingredients with measured amounts are included, but ingredients without specific quantities are not.

* If a whole accompanying recipe (such as for a sauce) is listed as "for serving," it is not included in the analysis. But the sauce's recipe will have its macros listed there.

my protein-powered kitchen

pantry staples

Every good cook has their own selection of kitchen staples. Over the years, these are the ingredients that I've gravitated toward the most . . . when I run out, I find myself immediately picking up my phone to see if I can order them for same-day delivery. (Yes, they are really that crucial!) These ingredients form the backbone of many of my recipes, and having them on hand will make it easier to cook your way through this book. You don't necessarily need everything on this list—trust your own taste first—but these are my personal go-tos.

Diamond Crystal Kosher Salt

This is the salt I use in all my recipes, and I recommend you do the same. Diamond Crystal Kosher Salt has a light, flaky texture and a lower density, making it slightly less "salty" than other table salts—which I like because it gives you more control when seasoning. If you are using a different type or brand of salt—Morton Kosher or another table salt—use one-third to one-half the amount called for in the recipes, or just salt to your taste.

Spices

I keep a very wide variety of spices in my cabinet at all times. Probably a lot bigger than most people. I prefer to buy Simply Organic brand spices because they are stored in glass bottles and come from organic plants. The spices I use most often are black pepper, garlic powder, onion powder, paprika, smoked paprika, chili powder, dry ground mustard, oregano, basil, cumin, and cinnamon.

Oils

Extra-virgin olive oil and sesame oil are my most-used oils. Sesame oil I use sparingly, for its unique flavor. And to me, extra-virgin olive oil is super versatile; some people say it's not for sautéing or you can't cook with it, but it's all I really use. The only thing I look for when it comes to buying olive oil, is buying one that comes in a dark-colored glass bottle (which helps keep sunlight from changing its flavor) and making sure it is 100 percent olive oil. I like to buy it in bulk at Costco and refill my own smaller bottle.

Vinegars

I didn't use a ton of vinegars when I first started cooking, but over time, I've found they can help you create a great balance of flavors. If your dish is feeling a little too heavy, too bitter, or too boring, a splash of vinegar can help. My top three most used are red wine vinegar, balsamic vinegar, and seasoned rice vinegar.

Seasoning Blends

I have no shame in using seasoning blends. They exist for a reason—they can add different flavor profiles to foods quickly and it makes cooking simple, healthy meals really easy. Some of my absolute must-haves are Lawry's Garlic Salt with Parsley, Fire & Smoke Society's Black & Tan steak rub, Gibsons Steakhouse Seasoning Salt, Old Bay seasoning, a chile-lime seasoning (like Tajín), and a Cajun and a Creole seasoning blend (like Tony Chachere's).

Sweeteners

I have all kinds of sweeteners, and each has its purpose. The ones I use the most are brown sugar erythritol (low-carb, such as Swerve) or monk fruit sweetener (no-carb), honey (regular and hot), and maple syrup.

Bone Broths and Stocks

I sometimes wish I was one of those cooks who makes their own stocks and broths, but let's be honest—I'm not, and I'm not sure I ever will be. Because of that, I always keep Better than Bouillon pastes—in Chicken and Beef flavors—in my fridge at all times so I can have broth on hand at a moment's notice. If I need to bump up the protein in a dish, I'll swap in store-bought beef or chicken bone broth.

fridge staples

Salted Butter
I very rarely use unsalted butter. Kerrygold butter never fails me, but whatever butter you end up buying, just make sure it is in fact real butter (not the fake hydrogenated oil stuff).

Sugar-Free Condiments
There are so many good sugar-free options for BBQ sauce and ketchup, so I really only buy sugar-free ones. My favorites are Heinz no-sugar-added ketchup and the entire G Hughes Sugar Free BBQ Sauce line—they're amazing!

Mustards
I use mustard pretty often in my cooking. I like to put Dijon in dressings and marinades, but I sometimes use yellow mustard for dips.

Light Mayonnaise
Mayo is one of those things that you either love or hate. I love it— I actually can't live without it. Regular mayo is amazing, but it's so heavy in calories, so I opt for light mayo most of the time (though either will work if you only have a regular version on hand). My favorite brands are Hellmann's and Duke's.

Sauces
I go through coconut aminos like nobody's business. It's mostly sold as a soy-free soy sauce alternative. It's one of my favorite ingredients to use in a marinade for meat or to add a soy-like umami flavor to any dish. Since I use so much of it, I like to buy big bottles on Amazon. I also use a lot of pesto—when buying pesto, I just make sure it is made with olive oil, not seed oil. I also always keep Japanese bbq sauce and salsa on hand. I like to buy the homemade salsas from Petes— one of my local grocery stores.

Pickled Foods
I have an entire shelf in my fridge dedicated to pickled things. One of my favorites is classic dill pickles, of course, but I also use a lot of banana peppers, hot chili peppers, giardiniera, olives, and pickled red onions. When I feel like a dish is missing something, adding a pickled element often makes all the difference.

Dairy
I use Greek yogurt, Parmesan cheese, and cottage cheese in a ton of recipes. If you hate Greek yogurt, you can often sub it out for sour cream. I personally love using Greek yogurt since it adds so much protein—my favorite brand is FAGE. My favorite brands of cottage cheese are Good Culture and Kalona Farms SuperNatural. I'm not picky with Parmesan.

Spicy Stuff
If you're not a fan of spicy food, you might want to skip these, but when I'm looking to add some heat to a dish, I keep a variety of options on hand. My go-tos are hot sauces like Cholula, Louisiana, Truff hot sauce, and Sriracha, along with garlic chili crisp, canned chipotle peppers in adobo sauce, and Calabrian chili peppers in oil. Each brings its own unique kick and depth of flavor to elevate any dish.

Garlic, Ginger, and Green Onion
This is my holy trinity when it comes to cooking. While fresh garlic and ginger are always great, I honestly love using the frozen cubes made by Dorot— they're so convenient to pop out, they thaw quickly, and they save me from having to mince garlic or ginger. Plus, they're pre-measured! As an alternative to frozen garlic cubes, I sometimes also buy large wholesale bags of peeled garlic cloves, pulse them into a paste in a food processor, and then store them as flat as possible in a resealable ziplock bag. I divide it into portions by making indents with chopsticks or the blunt edge of a knife. Green onion is another staple for me; I go through at least one bunch a week, and you'll see it used often in this book.

Lemons and Limes
These are both great to have on hand and can elevate or brighten almost any dish. I always grab at least one lemon whenever I'm at the grocery store. I keep a bottle of lime juice on hand, which I love because it lasts a long time and it's perfect for a quick dressing or marinade.

equipment & tools

It's important to me to make cooking as smooth and effortless as possible—which means it's important to have the right tools on hand. I'm the kind of person who will travel with my essential cooking tools because they make such a difference for me in the kitchen. Choosing the right size items for your needs, investing in high-quality products, and keeping frequently used items easily accessible are key when setting up your kitchen.

Measuring spoons and cups

I don't know how I went so long without having a set of magnetic measuring spoons (as opposed to the ones that come on a ring). I found my set online, and they're so much easier to keep organized and all in one place.

Wooden cutting board (grooved, to catch juices)

I prefer wood to plastic cutting boards for the most part; they're gentler on your knives, look great, and are actually better than plastic at not trapping bacteria as long as you clean them well. Right now, my main cutting board is a large 18" x 12" Boos Block, but it's not something I think you need to splurge on right off the bat. For the longest time I used the same two affordable wooden cutting boards; I recommend having at least one larger-size grooved cutting board to rest and slice meat after cooking. Keep them maintained well with oil and they will last you years!

Disposable gloves (for handling meat)

I personally don't like touching raw meat, but if that's not an issue for you, you probably won't need these. I have long nails and think using gloves while handling raw meat is a little more sanitary. This is something I genuinely can't cook without anymore.

Blender

I have a large Vitamix blender and a smaller NutriBullet blender. I like to use my Vitamix for things like soups and smoothies, but having something smaller like a NutriBullet is very convenient for sauces, dips, and marinades.

Vegetable chopper

If you're someone who hates dicing and chopping, a vegetable chopper is a must-have addition to your kitchen. They work basically like a press—you use the lid to push large chunks of vegetables through a blade. It makes cutting so much quicker and easier for me, and they tend to come with a few types of blades depending on your needs. There are tons of options, but I personally use the Fullstar brand. It's essential for lazy cooks (like me)!

Baking sheets/sheet pans

I recommend having a variety of sizes of sheet pans/baking sheets. I keep a few smaller (quarter-size) 9 by 13-inch ones, and a couple of large ones (12 by 16 inches).

Slow cooker

I have a good handful of slow cooker recipes in this book. They are really convenient for meats that need to cook low and slow, and it's nice to forget about dinner for hours . . . and come back to a rich, well-developed dish.

Air fryer

I love my air fryer, and I use it often. Many of the recipes in this book were developed with an air fryer—you can sometimes use an oven in its place, but the quick, intense heat of the air fryer is preferable. I recommend any basket-style air fryer because they are the easiest to clean, heat up the food quicker than other kinds, and most importantly, make the crispiest food!

10- and 12-inch skillets

I personally use stainless steel for most of my cooking, but a non-stick pan will also work for these recipes. I prefer pans that are oven-safe, as there are a few recipes in here that need to transfer from stove to oven, but you can also transfer the food onto a size-appropriate sheet pan as well. I use a mix of Made-In stainless steel and ceramic pans.

Mixing bowls

I like to keep a full set of both glass and stainless-steel mixing bowls. If you only have room for one set, I would recommend glass ones because they are microwave safe and can be used for just about anything. I would recommend at least having a few small ones and one larger one if you don't want to buy a full set.

Long and short metal tongs

Wooden utensil set (spoons & spatulas) and silicone rubber spatulas

Wooden spoons and spatulas are a staple in my kitchen. They are non-toxic and gentle on cookware. I primarily use wood (or metal) when I can, but I also like to keep a few silicone spatulas to scrape out bowls and use sparingly on heat if needed.

Chef's knife

This is obviously a super-essential tool in the kitchen. Really, any knife that you are comfortable with will work. I most commonly use my 7-inch chef knife, and I keep it sharp with a honing rod regularly before use. Always be sure to wipe off the edge after sharpening.

Kitchen shears

I use my kitchen shears almost daily for random things like cutting parchment paper, twine, or for butchering and trimming any fat off meats. They differ from regular scissors because you can take them apart for a more thorough cleaning.

Mandolin or Y-shaped vegetable peeler

Use the peeler that feels most comfortable in your hand, but I feel that I get more control with Y-shaped peelers.

Instant-read thermometer

These are $10 online and worth every penny. If you are cooking a lot of meats, this is such an important tool to have to make sure you are cooking meat to the proper temperature.

Glass containers with lids

I use glass for storing meal prep and leftovers. I try to avoid using plastic for food storage—especially for food that's still hot—since plastic can leach into food. Glass is safer for reheating and is better for long-term use, keeping your food away from any leaching microplastics, phthalates, and general consequences of plastic degradation.

Parchment Paper Sheets

I always keep unbleached, pre-cut parchment paper sheets in the kitchen. Once you start buying them it is hard to go back. I buy them in both 12" x 8" and 12" x 16" sizes online in packs that last me awhile. They make clean-up so much easier.

eggs & dairy

Cottage cheese is one of my favorite protein "hacks." Growing up, I had zero interest in anything with cottage cheese—but thanks to social media, I've learned there are so many ways you can use it. That includes blending it into a protein-rich, carb-free batter for wraps or pancakes, like in this recipe. These wraps are made with just three ingredients, and each serving has 20 grams of protein! I love making BLT wraps, but this recipe is super versatile and can be used for anything you want to enjoy wrap-style!

blt cottage cheese egg wraps

1 cup whole-milk cottage cheese

2 large eggs

1 tablespoon store-bought pesto

2 tablespoons light mayonnaise

4 slices center cut bacon, fully cooked

2 Roma tomatoes, thinly sliced

Handful of fresh arugula or fresh herbs, like basil or chives

2 teaspoons balsamic glaze

Kosher salt

Freshly ground black pepper

1. Preheat the oven to 425°F. Line a quarter sheet pan with parchment paper.

2. In a blender, combine the cottage cheese, eggs, and pesto. Blend until smooth, about 1 minute. Pour the mixture onto the lined sheet pan and use a spatula to spread it out evenly in a large rectangle, filling the whole sheet pan.

3. Bake until the cottage cheese mixture is set (the bottom should be golden brown), about 30 minutes. Remove from the oven and let cool for a few minutes.

4. Once the egg "wrap" is cool enough to handle, slice it in half. Spread each half with a light layer of mayo, and top with bacon, tomato, arugula, and balsamic glaze. Season with salt and pepper.

5. Roll up into wraps and serve!

Makes 2 servings * Total time: about 35 minutes
Per serving * Calories: 340 * Protein: 25g * Carbohydrates: 12g * Fat: 12g

For the longest time, these bacon cheddar egg bites were hands-down my favorite thing to meal prep for breakfast (they freeze and reheat beautifully). Adding cottage cheese bumps up the protein, but it also makes the egg bites super creamy and soft on the inside. For me, nothing tops classic bacon and cheese, but some other combinations I've enjoyed are ham with shredded Swiss, turkey bacon with spinach, and chicken sausage with bell pepper and feta.

bacon cheddar egg bites

Olive oil cooking spray

8 slices center cut bacon, cooked, then chopped

4 ounces cheddar cheese, shredded

6 green onions, green tops only, thinly sliced

8 large eggs

1½ cups whole-milk cottage cheese

½ teaspoon hot sauce

¼ teaspoon kosher salt

1. Preheat the oven to 375°F.

2. Grease 12 cups of a standard muffin tin with cooking spray. Place the bacon, cheddar, and green onions into each muffin cup, evenly divided.

3. In a blender, combine the eggs, cottage cheese, hot sauce, and salt. Blend until smooth and well combined.

4. Pour the egg mixture into the muffin cups, filling them about three-quarters of the way. Use chopsticks or a small spoon to mix the filling around to ensure the eggs and filling are incorporated.

5. Transfer to the oven and bake until the eggs are set, about 15 minutes.

6. Remove from the oven and allow the egg bites to cool in the pan for 1 to 2 minutes, then use a small silicone spatula to remove them from the muffin tin. Enjoy immediately or transfer to a plate or glass container for storing.

Makes 12 egg bites (6 servings) ⋆ **Total time:** about 20 minutes
Per serving ⋆ **Calories:** 280 ⋆ **Protein:** 22g ⋆ **Carbohydrates:** 4g ⋆ **Fat:** 19g

I used to love to go to a restaurant called Fire + Wine in Glen Ellyn, Illinois. They served an incredible dish with whipped ricotta and fresh honeycomb on warm bread. I don't live near Fire + Wine anymore, but I wanted to create an ode to the dish—and up the protein. The ingredients used in my version are accessible and affordable, and I designed the dish to work as a meal rather than just an appetizer. The prosciutto adds a nice saltiness, too. Possibly my favorite thing about this meal is that it comes together in 10 minutes from start to finish. You can easily prep the whipped ricotta ahead of time, and I recommend making extra so you have leftovers for a couple of days. For the toast, I like to use a sourdough, but a crusty baguette would make a nice alternative as well.

whipped ricotta toast
with prosciutto

1½ cups whole-milk ricotta cheese

¼ cup whole-milk Greek yogurt

1 tablespoon honey

¼ teaspoon kosher salt

4 slices sourdough bread

8 slices prosciutto

1. In a food processor, combine the ricotta, yogurt, honey, and salt. Process on high speed until the ricotta mixture is smooth and well combined, 1 to 2 minutes.

2. Toast the bread to your preference.

3. Spread the whipped ricotta mixture on the toasts, top each toast with 2 slices of prosciutto, and serve immediately.

Makes 4 servings * **Total time:** about 10 minutes
Per serving * **Calories:** 410 * **Protein:** 25g * **Carbohydrates:** 36g * **Fat:** 19g

In the process of dreaming up creative ways to use protein powder (other than the usual shake or smoothie), one of my favorite desserts kept coming to mind: banana pudding. I added powdered peanut butter to the mix and ended up with a pudding that is out of this world! I'm completely hooked on it—bananas and peanut butter are my favorite flavor combo. Including chia seeds, which are high in fiber and omega-3 fatty acids, helps this recipe keep me full for a long time. If you don't love the texture of chia pudding—I didn't at first—you can grind the chia seeds in a blender before adding them for a smoother consistency. This pudding is also perfect for meal prep, especially if you like to start your morning with something sweet!

banana nut chia seed pudding

1 cup whole milk

1 cup whole-milk Greek yogurt

2 scoops vanilla protein powder

2 ripe bananas, sliced and frozen

¼ teaspoon vanilla extract

¼ cup powdered peanut butter

Pinch kosher salt

½ cup chia seeds

For Serving
¼ cup chopped walnuts

1. In a blender, combine the milk, yogurt, protein powder, bananas, vanilla, powdered peanut butter, and salt. Blend until smooth.

2. Transfer the mixture to four 16-ounce glass containers with lids, and add 2 tablespoons of chia seeds to each container. Stir well. Cover and refrigerate overnight, or for at least 2 hours.

3. To serve, top each chia seed pudding with 1 tablespoon of chopped walnuts.

tip: You can make lots of different versions of this using any other favorite fruit—just use milk, yogurt, and vanilla protein powder as a base.

Makes 4 servings ＊ **Total time:** about 2 hours, most of it chilling time
Per serving ＊ **Calories:** 370 ＊ **Protein:** 23g ＊ **Carbohydrates:** 31g ＊ **Fat:** 19g

Once, on a trip to the Florida Keys, my boyfriend, Joe, and I stayed at a resort that served these amazing breakfast tostadas, made with crispy carnitas and a poached runny egg on top. I became obsessed with tostadas after that, and they've become one of my go-to weekend meals ever since. I use my own Simple Pulled Pork (see Note on page 194) in place of carnitas and an avocado mash for some creaminess. Feel free to switch up the toppings to make it your own. I jump between pico de gallo, pickled carrots, and cheese. Try serving with a dollop of Chipotle Yogurt Sauce (page 40) and a slice of lime for brightness!

breakfast tostadas

1 avocado

Kosher salt (optional)

Lime juice (optional)

4 large eggs

4 tostada shells

8 ounces Simple Pulled Pork (see Note on page 194)

For Serving

2 ounces queso fresco, crumbled

2 tablespoons chopped fresh cilantro

2 tablespoons finely chopped red onion

Hot sauce

1. Preheat the oven to 400°F. Line a sheet pan with parchment paper.

2. In a small bowl, mash the avocado until smooth. You can add a pinch of salt and a squeeze of lime juice if desired for extra flavor. Set aside.

3. Poach the eggs: Fill a medium saucepan with about 3 inches of water (or enough to completely submerge the eggs) and bring to a very gentle simmer over medium heat. Crack each egg into a very small glass bowl or ramekin. One at a time, carefully lower the eggs into the saucepan, submerging most of the ramekin to ensure the egg whites stay intact, then tip the eggs in and remove the ramekin. Let the eggs poach until the whites are fully set but the yolks remain runny, about 4 minutes. Use a slotted spoon to carefully remove each poached egg from the water and place it on a paper towel to drain. Work in batches if needed.

4. Place the tostada shells on the lined sheet pan and bake for 5 minutes, until lightly toasted.

5. Assemble the tostadas: Spread a layer of mashed avocado evenly over each tostada shell. Top with 2 ounces of pork and 1 poached egg. Sprinkle the tostadas with queso fresco, cilantro, and red onion. Finish with hot sauce to taste and serve immediately.

Makes 4 tostadas * **Total time:** about 15 minutes
Per tostada * **Calories:** 370 * **Protein:** 21g * **Carbohydrates:** 16g * **Fat:** 26g

Oh, deviled eggs . . . I love you. I have been making this recipe for years, and I've never gotten tired of it. There are many ways to make deviled eggs—this is mine. I always like to put at least one pickled item on top, my favorite being jalapeños. To take it one step further, I add eggs' best friend—bacon—because, well, why not? These are a festive snack for a holiday party and are also great to have on hand for a quick snack. And sure, why not for breakfast, too?

bacon & jalapeño deviled eggs

8 large Hard-Boiled Eggs (page 45)

¼ cup light mayonnaise

2 teaspoons Dijon mustard

2 teaspoons pickled jalapeño brine

¼ teaspoon kosher salt

4 slices center cut bacon, cooked, then crumbled

16 slices pickled jalapeño

1. Using a sharp knife, halve the hard-boiled eggs lengthwise, wiping the knife after each egg to ensure a clean cut. Use a small spoon to scoop the yolks into a small mixing bowl, and set the whites aside. Add the mayo, mustard, jalapeño brine, and salt to the egg yolks and stir until well combined.

2. Use a small spoon or spatula to transfer the mixture to a small resealable ziplock bag. Cut off a small corner of the bag to create a makeshift piping bag, then pipe the yolk mixture into the egg white halves.

3. Arrange the deviled eggs on a serving tray. Sprinkle the deviled eggs with crumbled bacon and top each egg with a slice of pickled jalapeño.

note: If you're not into spicy pickled foods, you can still buy pickled jalapeños without the spice. Look for the jar that says "tamed" jalapeños instead of "hot" or "mild."

Makes 4 servings (16 pieces) ∗ **Total time:** about 35 minutes
Per serving ∗ **Calories:** 220 ∗ **Protein:** 15g ∗ **Carbohydrates:** 3g ∗ **Fat:** 16g

Growing up, my mom always made chorizo and eggs, and it was one of my and my brothers' favorite breakfasts. We all ate it a little differently—my older brother eating it with ripped-up slices of white bread, my little brother likely dousing it in ketchup, and me, eating it as a taco on corn tortillas. These days, I like to turn this breakfast classic into a casserole. I sneak in some extra protein by adding my favorite protein hack—cottage cheese. This is a great pick for a weekend brunch moment, but it also works as meal prep for breakfast throughout the week. If you don't have any chipotle peppers in adobo sauce on hand to make the Chipotle Yogurt Sauce, you can still serve with plain sour cream or Greek yogurt.

chorizo egg bake

Olive oil cooking spray

8 large eggs

1½ cups whole-milk cottage cheese

1 teaspoon kosher salt

12 ounces Mexican-style chorizo

6 ounces Chihuahua-style melting cheese, Monterey Jack, mozzarella, or cheddar Jack, shredded

Chipotle Yogurt Sauce, for serving (recipe follows)

1. Preheat the oven to 375°F. Grease a 9 by 13-inch baking dish with cooking spray.

2. Prepare the chorizo egg bake: In a blender, add the eggs, cottage cheese, and salt and blend until fully combined.

3. In a large skillet, cook the chorizo over medium heat, using a wooden spoon to stir and break apart any large pieces, until it's browned and cooked through, 5 to 7 minutes.

4. Transfer the cooked chorizo to a fine-mesh sieve and set it over the pan. Let the grease drip back into the pan, gently pressing the chorizo with the back of a spoon to release any excess grease.

5. Transfer the chorizo to the prepared baking dish, top with the cheese, and pour the egg mixture on top. Using a wooden spoon, gently stir the egg mixture into the chorizo and cheese to incorporate.

6. Transfer to the oven and bake until the eggs are fully set and the top begins to turn golden brown, about 40 minutes. In the meantime, prepare the Chipotle Yogurt Sauce.

7. Remove from the oven and let the casserole cool for 5 minutes before slicing. Serve with a dollop of Chipotle Yogurt Sauce.

(recipe continues)

serving suggestions *
Cut the casserole into thin slices and serve on a tortilla, taco style, or eat on top of a crispy hashbrown patty (store-bought or homemade).

Makes 6 servings * **Total time:** about 1 hour
Per serving, not including sauce * **Calories:** 400 * **Protein:** 31g *
Carbohydrates: 5g * **Fat:** 28g

Chipotle Yogurt Sauce * Makes about 1 cup (8 servings)

¾ cup whole-milk
Greek yogurt

¼ cup light mayonnaise

Juice of 1 lime

2 whole chipotle peppers
in adobo sauce

1 teaspoon honey

¼ teaspoon kosher salt

In a food processor or blender, combine the yogurt, mayonnaise, lime juice, chipotle peppers, honey, salt, and ¼ cup water. Blend until fully combined. Transfer to an airtight container and refrigerate until ready to use. It will keep in the fridge for up to 1 week.

Per 2 tablespoons * Calories: 30 * Protein: 1g * Carbohydrates: 2g * Fat: 1.5g

If you've ever wanted to stir the pot on the Internet, just add grape jelly to your breakfast sandwich! This freezer-friendly breakfast sandwich recipe caused an absolute frenzy when I first shared it on social media, with people asking me how I could possibly like the taste of grape jelly with sausage, bacon, and eggs. And my response is: Don't knock it 'til you try it! If you really think about it, what's not to like? People eat bacon with maple syrup–drenched pancakes all the time, right? It's not so different.

Try this recipe with grape jelly at least once—heck, use any jelly you'd like— and if it's still not for you, so be it. But trust me, I think you'll like it more than you expect. (If you're *really* not inclined to try the jelly, okay, okay, do a little bit of guacamole instead.)

Condiment drama aside, the star of these sandwiches is the homemade sweet and spicy sausage patty, which goes great with the egg, turkey bacon, and—trust me—grape jelly. I love making these as meal prep because they're pre-assembled, so I can take one out of the freezer the night before, thaw it in the fridge overnight, and it's ready to pop into the microwave or air fryer the next morning. You'll spend about an hour meal-prepping this one, but it's well worth it for a quick and easy breakfast that you can enjoy all week.

sweet & spicy breakfast sandwiches

12 slices turkey bacon

6 Sweet Heat Breakfast Sausage patties, cooked (see page 101)

6 multigrain English muffins, split

6 large eggs

Olive oil cooking spray

6 slices American cheese, preferably Kraft Deli Deluxe

For Serving

Grape jelly or guacamole (optional)

Hot sauce

1. Preheat the oven to 375°F. Line a sheet pan with parchment paper.

2. Arrange the turkey bacon on the sheet pan and bake in the oven until crispy, 10 to 12 minutes, flipping halfway through. Transfer the bacon to a plate and cover it with foil to keep it warm.

3. Wipe off the parchment paper with a paper towel to remove excess oil. Then, arrange the English muffins, split-sides up, on the same parchment. Bake until golden brown, 5 to 7 minutes. Cover with foil to keep warm and set aside. Leave the oven on.

(recipe continues)

Makes 6 sandwiches * **Total time:** about 1 hour
Per sandwich * **Calories:** 450 * **Protein:** 35g * **Carbohydrates:** 36g * **Fat:** 19g

storage/reheating

4. Make the eggs: Line a second sheet pan with parchment paper. Place 6 egg rings on the sheet pan and coat them with cooking spray. Carefully crack an egg into each ring, making sure the egg white is contained in the ring and the yolk stays intact. Cover the sheet pan tightly with aluminum foil.

5. Transfer the eggs to the oven and bake for 8 minutes, then remove the foil and continue baking until the egg whites are set and the yolks are still soft, about 2 more minutes.

6. Remove the sheet pan from the oven and use tongs to gently lift the egg rings. Use a spatula to remove the eggs from the pan.

7. Assemble the sandwiches: Place a sausage patty on the bottom half of each English muffin. Top with 2 slices of turkey bacon, 1 slice of American (cut the cheese to fit the English muffin), and an egg. Close each sandwich with the top half. (If meal prepping, see Storage/Reheating.)

8. To serve, spread 1 to 2 tablespoons of grape jelly or guacamole on the inside of the top half of the English muffin. Serve with hot sauce and enjoy!

If you had told me just a few years ago that cottage cheese would make a huge comeback, I definitely wouldn't have believed you. But take one look at social media and you'll see that cottage cheese has become the star of the show. Cottage cheese "power bowls" are just one example.

There are many ways to make this bowl your own—for instance, you can drizzle it with hot honey or garlic chili crisp oil and sprinkle it with green onions. I encourage you to get creative with this dish, and tell your mom or grandma you like cottage cheese—they'll be so surprised and hopefully impressed!

cottage cheese breakfast bowls

4 large Jammy Eggs
(see below)

1 cup whole-milk
cottage cheese

½ cup thinly sliced
mini cucumbers

½ cup cherry
tomatoes, halved

4 slices center cut bacon,
cooked, then chopped

4 green onions, green
tops only, thinly slice

Place ½ cup cottage cheese in two bowls. Quarter the eggs and arrange them on top of the cottage cheese. Top with the cucumbers, cherry tomatoes, bacon, and green onion and serve.

Makes 2 servings ⋆ **Total time:** about 10 minutes
Per serving ⋆ **Calories:** 340 ⋆ **Protein:** 31g ⋆ **Carbohydrates:** 9g ⋆ **Fat:** 21g

Jammy or Hard–Boiled Eggs ⋆ Makes as many as you need

Large eggs

1. Fill a small pot with enough water to almost cover the eggs by about three-quarters once you place them in there. Bring to a boil.

2. For jammy eggs: Once the water is boiling, use a spoon to carefully lower the eggs into the pot. Reduce the heat to a gentle simmer, cover the pot, and set a timer for 6 minutes. After 6 minutes turn off the heat, keeping the pot covered. Leave the eggs in the hot water for an additional 1 to 2 minutes, depending on how jammy you like the yolks.

3. For hard-boiled eggs: Once the water in the pot is boiling, carefully lower the eggs into the pot. Reduce the heat to a gentle simmer, cover, and set a timer for 12 minutes. Fill a bowl with ice water and set aside. After 12 minutes, turn off the heat, keeping the pot covered for an additional 2 minutes, then transfer the eggs to the ice bath for 2 to 3 minutes before peeling.

Let's make the creamy dill egg salad of your dreams. I'm not reinventing the wheel here—though I do use cottage cheese instead of mayo for more protein, and I add mustard and pickle brine for flavor. I like to eat this on the crispiest possible cracker instead of on a sandwich—I like the crunch—but of course, you do you. This is a quick and easy recipe, especially if you have hard-boiled eggs ready in the fridge. I love to meal prep the whole thing ahead of time for a quick lunch.

creamy dill egg salad

8 large Hard-Boiled Eggs (page 45)

1 cup whole-milk cottage cheese

1 tablespoon Dijon mustard

2 tablespoons pickle brine

1 tablespoon minced fresh chives

½ teaspoon dried dill

Kosher salt

Freshly ground black pepper

For Serving

4 slices multigrain crispbread, such as Wasa

1. Peel and finely dice the eggs and transfer to a mixing bowl. To the same bowl, add the cottage cheese, mustard, pickle brine, chives, dill, and salt and pepper to taste. Mix with a wooden spoon or spatula until combined.

2. Spoon the egg salad onto each crispbread, spreading in an even layer, and serve immediately.

serving suggestion * For a "melt" variation, spread the egg salad on a slice of bread, top with a slice of cheese (cheddar or pepper Jack would work great), and bake in the oven at 350°F until the cheese is melted, bubbling, and lightly browned.

Makes 2 servings * **Total time:** about 20 minutes
Per serving * **Calories:** 510 * **Protein:** 42g * **Carbohydrates:** 31g * **Fat:** 24g

fan favorite!

This one-pan egg-and-cheese breakfast quesadilla was one of the first recipes I posted on social media that really gained me some traction. It was my first video to hit one million views! Looking back at it now, the video isn't the best quality, but the quesadilla itself looked great, and that's all that matters.

I've continued to make this recipe over the years because it's a quick and easy breakfast idea that just never gets old. I love to use chicken chorizo sausage here, but you could easily replace it with turkey bacon, pork sausage, or even steak to change things up. If you want to sneak in some greens, whisk some finely chopped green onions into the eggs. This goes great with my Chipotle Yogurt Sauce (page 40), and I sometimes also add hot sauce for a spicy finish that brings all the flavors together.

one-pan breakfast quesadillas

4 large eggs

1 tablespoon salted butter

2 (10-inch) low-carb flour tortillas

¼ cup Chihuahua-style melting cheese, shredded

4 ounces Mexican-style chorizo or breakfast sausage, cooked and crumbled

¼ cup Chipotle Yogurt Sauce (page 40)

1. In a small bowl, whisk the eggs until fully combined and frothy.

2. Set a small nonstick skillet over medium-low heat. Add ½ tablespoon of the butter, let it melt, and swirl it around to coat the bottom of the pan. Pour in half of the whisked eggs and let them cook undisturbed until the edges begin to set, about 1 minute. Using a spatula, nudge the cooked edges into the center and let the eggs continue cooking for an additional 2 minutes, until almost fully set.

3. Place a tortilla on top of the almost-cooked eggs. Slide a large heatproof spatula under the eggs and carefully flip them to begin toasting the tortilla (the eggs should now be facing up).

4. Place half of the cheese and chorizo on one side of the eggs, then use the spatula to fold the tortilla in half. Continue cooking for about 1 minute on each side, or until the tortilla is golden brown and the egg is set. Repeat to make a second quesadilla. Serve hot with Chipotle Yogurt Sauce for dipping.

Makes 2 quesadillas ⋆ **Total time:** about 20 minutes
Per quesadilla ⋆ **Calories:** 520 ⋆ **Protein:** 36g ⋆ **Carbohydrates:** 9g ⋆ **Fat:** 36g

If you're a fan of bagels with lox and other fixings, you're guaranteed to love this. It's my slightly lower-calorie, higher-protein take on the classic bagel and lox, and it's so good and so easy to whip up. I use an English muffin in place of a bagel and a mixture of cream cheese blended with cottage cheese. The richness still comes through, but it's also loaded up with protein, and the lemon, capers, and red onion add plenty of flavor. I use smoked salmon for this recipe because it's easier to find than lox (which is cured but unsmoked salmon), but you can use either one.

loaded english muffins
with smoked salmon

2 multigrain English muffins, split

¼ cup cream cheese

½ cup whole-milk cottage cheese

½ teaspoon fresh lemon juice

2 tablespoons minced capers

6 ounces thinly sliced smoked salmon

¼ cup thinly sliced cucumber

¼ red onion, thinly sliced

1 teaspoon everything bagel seasoning

1. Toast the English muffins until golden brown.

2. **Meanwhile, make the cream cheese mixture:** In a food processor or small blender, combine the cream cheese, cottage cheese, and lemon juice and purée until smooth and whipped.

3. Spread a spoonful of the cream cheese mixture on each English muffin half. Top each half with 1 tablespoon of capers, followed by the smoked salmon, cucumber, and red onions. Sprinkle with everything bagel seasoning and serve!

tip: If meal prepping, you can easily make a double batch of the cream cheese mixture to have ready for an easy weekday breakfast.

Makes 2 servings * Total time: about 10 minutes
Per serving * Calories: 420 * Protein: 29g * Carbohydrates: 33g * Fat: 19g

This is probably another recipe where you wouldn't expect cottage cheese to feature, but it's really that versatile! This recipe uses cottage cheese for a delicious, high-protein pancake. These aren't going to be the fluffiest pancakes in the world; they're more like a thick, sweet crepe. If you don't have oats on hand, you can swap them out for ¼ cup of regular flour, which will give the pancakes a fluffier consistency.

maple cinnamon pancakes

1 cup whole-milk cottage cheese

2 large eggs

½ cup rolled oats

1 scoop vanilla protein powder

2 tablespoons whole milk

1 teaspoon vanilla extract

1 tablespoon maple syrup

2 teaspoons baking powder

½ teaspoon cinnamon

Pinch kosher salt

2 tablespoons salted butter, for frying

For Serving
Whipped cream (optional)
Maple syrup (optional)

1. In a blender or food processor, combine the cottage cheese, eggs, rolled oats, protein powder, milk, vanilla, maple syrup, baking powder, cinnamon, and salt. Blend until the mixture is well combined with a smooth consistency.

2. Set a nonstick skillet or griddle over medium heat. Melt ½ teaspoon of butter in the skillet and swirl to coat the pan. Pour about ¼ cup of pancake batter onto the skillet and cook until bubbles form and the edges start to set, 1 to 2 minutes. Repeat to make additional pancakes, but be careful to avoid crowding the skillet.

3. Carefully flip the pancakes using a sturdy spatula. Cook on the other side for 1 to 2 more minutes, or until golden brown. Transfer the finished pancakes to a warmed plate to keep them hot.

4. Repeat with the remaining batter, adding more butter to the skillet as needed. Serve the pancakes hot, with whipped cream and more maple syrup if desired.

serving suggestions ＊
Serve with a side of fresh berries.

Makes 2 servings (about 8 pancakes) ＊ **Total time:** about 20 minutes
Per serving ＊ **Calories:** 440 ＊ **Protein:** 38g ＊ **Carbohydrates:** 28g ＊ **Fat:** 23g

poultry

I had quite a few jobs before I became a social media content creator, and one of those jobs was at a sports bar that was known for their wings. They had probably over twenty options on the menu, but my favorite was the garlic Parmesan. This is my spin on it.

I probably saw thousands of orders of wings go out of that kitchen, and yet, wings are still one of my favorite foods. I use baking powder to slightly "puff" the skin while the chicken is in the oven, which gets it extra crispy without frying.

This is one of the first recipes I ever posted on social media. Over eighteen million people viewed it, shared it, and raved about it, which was so exciting for me. I wanted to put it in this book because social media could disappear tomorrow, but this book will still be here.

roasted garlic–parmesan chicken wings

2½ pounds chicken wings, split into drumettes and flats

2 teaspoons garlic salt

1 teaspoon dried parsley

1 teaspoon baking powder

1 tablespoon extra-virgin olive oil

Garlic-Parmesan Sauce

3 tablespoons salted butter

2 teaspoons garlic salt

½ teaspoon red pepper flakes

¼ cup grated Parmesan cheese

1. Preheat the oven to 400°F. Line a large sheet pan with parchment paper.

2. In a large bowl, toss together the chicken wings, garlic salt, parsley, baking powder, and olive oil. Mix until the wings are fully coated.

3. Place the wings on the prepared sheet pan, with the side with thicker skin facing up. Transfer to the oven and roast for 25 minutes. Use tongs to flip the chicken wings and continue roasting for 25 more minutes. Flip the chicken wings one last time and continue roasting until both sides are very crispy and golden brown, about 5 minutes. Remove the wings from the oven and let rest for 2 minutes.

4. Meanwhile, make the garlic-Parmesan sauce: In a medium microwave-safe bowl, microwave the butter for 1 minute until fully melted.

5. Add the garlic salt, red pepper flakes, and Parmesan to the melted butter and stir to combine.

6. Place the wings in a large bowl and toss them in the garlic-Parmesan sauce until coated. Serve hot.

Makes 4 servings * Total time: about 1 hour
Per serving * Calories: 410 * Protein: 28g * Carbohydrates: 1g * Fat: 32g

This is a dish that I think is worth a little bit of a splurge—I usually get an organic, free-range chicken. For this recipe, you're going to spatchcock the chicken, which means cutting out the backbone of the chicken so it can lie flat while cooking. If you follow me on social media, you know this is my favorite way to roast a whole chicken: It helps the meat cook much more quickly and evenly for a tender, juicy finished product. Plus, the skin gets good and crispy as it roasts, since it's slathered in butter with rosemary and garlic. I love to make this meal on a Sunday, and I add any leftover chicken to salads during the week. I reheat leftover dark meat, like thighs and drumsticks, in the air fryer.

You can also use the spatchcocking technique on your Thanksgiving turkey for a delicious, time-saving twist! (If you have high-quality kitchen shears, you can do it yourself; but you can also ask the butcher to spatchcock it for you.)

I know cooking a whole chicken feels intimidating, but with practice, I promise you'll see how easy it really is. You can have a delicious meal on the table in just over an hour.

rosemary–lemon pepper
whole roast chicken

1 (3-pound) whole chicken

1 teaspoon lemon pepper seasoning

1 teaspoon kosher salt

¼ cup salted butter

2 teaspoons minced fresh rosemary

2 teaspoons minced garlic

¼ teaspoon ground turmeric

1 teaspoon honey

1 tablespoon extra-virgin olive oil

1. Position a rack in the bottom third of the oven and preheat the oven to 375°F. Line a sheet pan with parchment paper.

2. To spatchcock the chicken: Place the chicken breast-side down on a large cutting board. Using sturdy kitchen shears, cut along both sides of the backbone to remove it. Remove any innards that are stuck on the inside of the chicken if necessary. Open the chicken up and flip it over. Press down firmly on the breastbone to flatten the chicken as much as possible, as though you were pressing down on an open book to make it lie flat.

3. Transfer the chicken to the prepared sheet pan, breast-side up. Season all over with the lemon pepper seasoning and salt.

serving suggestion ★ This chicken pairs well with Garlic Cauliflower Mash (page 232).

Makes 4 servings ★ **Total time:** about 1 hour 15 minutes
Per serving ★ **Calories:** 530 ★ **Protein:** 44g ★ **Carbohydrates:** 2g ★ **Fat:** 37g

4. In a small glass bowl, microwave the butter for 30 seconds until melted. Add the rosemary, garlic, turmeric, honey, and olive oil to the bowl and stir until well combined. Brush the chicken all over with the butter mixture.

5. Transfer the chicken to the oven and roast until the internal temperature of the thigh meat reaches at least 175°F, about 1 hour. Tent the chicken with aluminum foil and let it rest for 10 to 15 minutes before carving.

6. Carve the chicken on a large wooden cutting board (with grooves to catch the juices). Serve immediately.

note: The USDA recommends an internal temperature of 165°F for fully cooked chicken, but I find that taking it up to 175°F creates more tender dark meat (which is my favorite part). It's kind of similar to meat that needs to be slow-cooked. If you want to prioritize the breast meat, though, reduce the cooking time to about 45 minutes and stop at 165°F.

Anytime somebody tells me they just got an air fryer and aren't sure what to cook first, I tell them to try chicken thighs. There are two great things about this recipe: One, it's incredibly quick—you really won't find a faster technique to making chicken thighs with crispy skin and tender, fall-off-the-bone meat. And two, you can make this recipe with any of your favorite seasoning combinations. I like to use a little bit of sugar in my seasoning to create a nice crust on the chicken. I also go heavy with onion and garlic and three different sources of heat, and I season pretty generously. You can adapt the seasonings as you like.

With any bone-in dark meat, I always recommend cooking a little beyond 165°F, which is the standard safe cooking temperature. In this case, I personally like to cook until the internal temperature reads about 185°F–200°F. I don't worry about the thighs getting dry because they're so juicy, and in my opinion, the higher temperature actually makes the meat more tender.

louisiana hot honey air-fryer chicken thighs

4 (6-ounce) bone-in, skin-on chicken thighs

1 teaspoon Swerve brown sugar erythritol

1 tablespoon paprika

1 tablespoon garlic salt

1½ teaspoons onion powder

½ teaspoon freshly ground black pepper

½ teaspoon cayenne pepper

¼ teaspoon dried thyme

1 tablespoon extra-virgin olive oil

½ tablespoon salted butter

2 tablespoons Louisiana brand hot sauce

2 tablespoons hot honey

1. Pat the chicken thighs dry with a paper towel.

2. Make the dry rub: In a small bowl, stir together the Swerve, paprika, garlic salt, onion powder, black pepper, cayenne, and thyme.

3. Preheat the air fryer to 375°F.

4. Trim any excess skin or fat off the thighs—you want to avoid too much skin hanging off of the chicken. Use a sharp knife to make a cut along each side of the bone on the flesh side of the thighs to make more room for the seasoning.

5. Place the chicken thighs on a large cutting board and coat them with the olive oil. Generously sprinkle three-quarters of the dry rub over both sides of the chicken thighs, using your hands to press the spices into the meat. Reserve the rest of the dry rub to season again later.

(recipe continues)

Makes 4 servings ★ **Total time:** about 35 minutes
Per serving ★ **Calories:** 310 ★ **Protein:** 23g ★ **Carbohydrates:** 12g ★ **Fat:** 19g

serving suggestion ★ For a complete meal requiring minimal effort, serve with steamed green beans and roasted or mashed potatoes.

6. Arrange the chicken thighs in the air-fryer basket in a single layer, skin-side down. Air-fry for 15 to 17 minutes.

7. Meanwhile, in a small microwave-safe bowl, combine the butter, hot sauce, and hot honey. Microwave for 15 seconds and stir until well combined.

8. Using tongs, carefully flip the chicken thighs so they're skin-side up. Lightly season the skin side with the leftover dry rub and return the chicken thighs to the air fryer. Reduce the heat to 350°F and continue air frying until the skin is crispy and golden brown and the thighs reach an internal temperature of 175° to 185°F, 5 to 7 minutes.

9. Let the chicken thighs rest for a few minutes, then coat them in the Louisiana hot honey sauce. Serve hot.

Remember that episode of *Seinfeld* where Elaine wanted the big salad? This is that: A hearty wedge-style salad that eats like a meal. This recipe offers a quick way to pan-sear the chicken, but if you're really short on time, you can also use meat from a store-bought rotisserie chicken. And who doesn't love a salad with plenty of cheese? Here, I create a low-carb crouton made from Parmesan cheese, which adds more protein to an already protein-packed meal.

In my humble opinion, the key to a good Caesar salad is homemade dressing and a lot of freshly ground black pepper. I use Greek yogurt as a base in my Caesar dressing because it's lower in fat and calories than mayonnaise but it's still super creamy. Of course, if a yogurt-based dressing isn't your thing, sub out the yogurt for your favorite mayonnaise. Enjoy!

chicken caesar wedge salad

⅓ cup grated Parmesan cheese (16 teaspoons)

2 heads romaine lettuce

2 (6-ounce) boneless, skinless chicken breasts

½ teaspoon kosher salt

¼ teaspoon freshly ground black pepper

1 tablespoon extra-virgin olive oil

Caesar Dressing

½ cup whole-milk Greek yogurt

2 tablespoons grated Parmesan cheese

2 tablespoons fresh lemon juice, plus more to taste

½ teaspoon Dijon mustard

1 tablespoon chopped capers

½ teaspoon anchovy paste

2 garlic cloves, minced

½ teaspoon kosher salt, plus more to taste

¼ teaspoon freshly ground black pepper, plus more to taste

1. Make the Parmesan croutons: Preheat the oven to 400°F. Line a large sheet pan with parchment paper.

2. Place small mounds of grated Parmesan cheese (about 2 teaspoons each) on the prepared sheet pan, leaving ample space between them. Flatten and spread each mound of cheese into a 3-inch round using the back of a spoon. Bake until the Parmesan is golden brown and crispy, 5 to 6 minutes.

(recipe continues)

Makes 4 servings ★ **Total time:** about 40 minutes
Per serving ★ **Calories:** 230 ★ **Protein:** 23g ★ **Carbohydrates:** 14g ★ **Fat:** 10g

3. Let the Parmesan crisps cool on the sheet pan for a few minutes until they are firm and crisp. Once cool enough to handle, break them into bite-size pieces and set aside.

4. Prep the lettuce: Rinse the romaine lettuce heads under cold running water, gently pulling back the leaves to remove any dirt or debris. Pat the lettuce dry with paper towels or a clean kitchen towel. Cut off and discard the root ends. Set aside.

5. Then, make the chicken: Season the chicken breasts with the salt and pepper. Set a skillet over medium-high heat and add the olive oil. Once hot, add the chicken breasts and cook until they are no longer pink in the center, 6 to 7 minutes per side (they should have an internal temperature of at least 165°F.) Remove the chicken breasts from the pan and set them aside to rest for a few minutes. Once cool enough to handle, slice them into bite-size pieces.

6. Make the Caesar dressing: In a medium bowl, whisk together the yogurt, Parmesan, lemon juice, mustard, capers, anchovy paste, garlic, salt, and pepper. Adjust the seasoning to taste. If the dressing is too thick, you can thin it with a little water or more lemon juice.

7. To assemble the salad, halve the romaine lettuce heads lengthwise to create 2 wedges per head. Place each wedge on a serving plate. Arrange sliced chicken on top of each lettuce wedge. Drizzle the Caesar dressing generously over the chicken and lettuce, then scatter the Parmesan croutons on top. Season with additional salt and pepper to taste and serve.

tip: If you love to grill and are feeling fancy, try grilling the romaine lettuce wedges to give them some flavorful char. Lightly oil the sides and put them on a hot grill for a minute or so, just until you get some nice grill lines and smoky flavor. The insides will still be crisp and refreshing.

Peri-peri chicken is a spicy Portuguese grilled chicken dish made famous around the world by a South African restaurant chain called Nando's. I've been making it for a long time in my own backyard on the grill. This recipe calls for a dry rub plus a marinade using the store-bought version of Nando's peri-peri sauce, which is made from vinegar, smoked paprika, chili powder, lemon, garlic, and coriander. If you can't find the real-deal, original Nando's sauce at your local grocery store, you can usually find it online, and Trader Joe's also carries a similar version.

peri-peri grilled chicken legs

2½ pounds chicken drumsticks

2 teaspoons kosher salt

2 teaspoons dried parsley

2 teaspoons paprika

1 teaspoon garlic powder

1 teaspoon onion powder

¼ teaspoon dried thyme

1 tablespoon extra-virgin olive oil

1 cup Nando's medium-hot peri-peri sauce

Neutral oil, for grill

For Serving
Chopped fresh parsley

1. **Butterfly the chicken drumsticks:** Using a sharp knife, cut along the length of each drumstick, slicing along each side of the bone to open up the meat. This will give you more surface area for seasoning and searing.

2. **Make the dry rub:** In a large bowl, combine the salt, dried parsley, paprika, garlic powder, onion powder, and thyme. Then add the olive oil and stir until well combined.

3. To the same bowl, add the butterflied drumsticks. Use your hands to toss them in the seasonings, ensuring they are well coated. Add ¾ cup of the peri-peri sauce to the bowl with the seasoned drumsticks, and toss to combine. Cover and marinate in the fridge for 4 hours.

4. Preheat the grill to medium-high heat and oil the grates.

5. Remove the drumsticks from the marinade and allow any excess liquid to drip off. Set the drumsticks on the grill grates and cover, opening to turn the drumsticks occasionally, until the chicken is fully cooked through, 15 to 20 minutes. During the last 5 minutes of grilling, brush the remaining ¼ cup of peri-peri sauce generously onto the drumsticks.

6. Let the drumsticks rest for a few minutes. Garnish with fresh parsley and serve hot.

serving suggestion ★
Serve with roasted carrots, Brussels sprouts, or red cabbage and a side salad to balance out the heat of the chicken. In the summertime, a tomato salad makes for a great side dish.

Makes 6 servings ★ Total time: about 45 minutes, plus 4 hours marinating time
Per serving ★ Calories: 250 ★ **Protein:** 23g ★ **Carbohydrates:** 1g ★ **Fat:** 12g

One of my favorite ways to prepare chicken breast is by stuffing it. These chicken breasts stuffed with an artichoke dip–like filling were a staple for me when I was on the keto diet, and I love it to this day. Stuffing the chicken breasts keeps them really juicy, partly because it doesn't take as long to cook them all the way through.

spinach artichoke–stuffed chicken

2 (6-ounce) boneless, skinless chicken breasts

½ teaspoon Italian seasoning

¼ teaspoon paprika

½ teaspoon kosher salt

½ cup cream cheese, at room temperature

½ cup chopped fresh spinach

¼ cup chopped marinated artichokes

2 tablespoons grated Parmesan cheese

2 garlic cloves, minced

¼ teaspoon red pepper flakes

1 tablespoon extra-virgin olive oil

1. Preheat the oven to 375°F.

2. Place the chicken breasts between two sheets of plastic wrap or parchment paper. Using a meat mallet, pound the thicker ends of the chicken breasts so they're about 1 inch thick.

3. Lay the pounded chicken breasts on a cutting board. Using a sharp knife, carefully make a horizontal slit along the side of each chicken breast, cutting about three-quarters of the way through to create a pocket for the stuffing.

4. Season both sides of the chicken breasts with Italian seasoning, paprika, and salt. Make sure to also season the inside of the "pockets."

5. Make the filling: In a medium bowl, combine the cream cheese, spinach, marinated artichokes, Parmesan, garlic, and red pepper flakes.

6. Spoon the filling mixture into the pockets you created in the chicken breasts. Press gently to pack the filling in.

7. Sear the chicken: Set an oven-safe skillet over medium-high heat and add the olive oil. Once hot, add the stuffed chicken and sear for 3 to 4 minutes per side, until just beginning to get golden brown.

8. Transfer the skillet to the oven and continue cooking until the chicken is fully golden brown and the internal temperature reaches 165°F, 15 to 20 minutes, depending on the size.

9. Remove the chicken breasts from the oven and let them rest for a few minutes. Carefully slice and serve hot.

tip: If you are short on time, a store-bought spinach and artichoke dip will work in this dish.

Makes 2 servings * **Total time:** about 45 minutes
Per serving * **Calories:** 490 * **Protein:** 40g * **Carbohydrates:** 7g * **Fat:** 33g

After I came home from college, I worked at a soup restaurant that served a caprese sandwich—and I became obsessed with the flavor combination of tomatoes, cheese, basil, and balsamic. Caprese is the inspiration for this recipe, and it's still one of my absolute favorites, but I love this higher-protein take.

This recipe is great any time of year, but it's best when you use ripe summer tomatoes. Pair with a simple green salad or roasted vegetables, like carrots, summer squash, sweet potatoes, or regular potatoes like Yukon Gold.

pesto-balsamic chicken caprese

Pesto-Balsamic Chicken (recipe follows)

5 Roma tomatoes, seeded and diced

½ shallot, minced

¼ cup minced fresh basil

2 garlic cloves, minced

1½ teaspoons balsamic vinegar

1½ teaspoons extra-virgin olive oil

Kosher salt

Freshly ground black pepper

½ cup whole-milk cottage cheese

2 teaspoons balsamic glaze

1. Prepare the Pesto-Balsamic Chicken.

2. **Make the tomato topping:** In a medium bowl, combine the tomatoes, shallot, basil, garlic, balsamic vinegar, olive oil, salt, and pepper. Stir well to combine.

3. Transfer the prepared chicken breasts to a serving platter. Spoon about 2 tablespoons of cottage cheese over each chicken breast, followed by the tomato topping. Drizzle with balsamic glaze and serve.

tip: If cottage cheese in this context isn't your thing, swap it out for shredded mozzarella and put it under a broiler until melted before covering the chicken in the tomato mixture and the glaze.

(recipe continues)

Makes 4 servings * **Total time:** about 50 minutes
Per serving * **Calories:** 470 * **Protein:** 50g * **Carbohydrates:** 12g * **Fat:** 25g

Pesto-Balsamic Chicken * Makes 4 servings

¼ cup extra-virgin olive oil

2 tablespoons balsamic vinegar

2 tablespoons store-bought pesto

1 tablespoon Swerve brown sugar erythritol

1 garlic clove, minced

2 teaspoons Italian seasoning

2 teaspoons kosher salt

¼ teaspoon freshly ground black pepper

4 (6-ounce) boneless, skinless chicken breasts

1. Make the marinade: In a small bowl, whisk together the olive oil, balsamic vinegar, pesto, Swerve, garlic, Italian seasoning, salt, and pepper.

2. Place the chicken breasts in a shallow dish or resealable ziplock bag and pour the marinade over the chicken, ensuring it is well coated. Cover or seal and refrigerate for at least 30 minutes, or up to 4 hours.

3. Set a grill pan over medium-high heat. While the grill pan heats up, remove the marinated chicken breasts from the fridge.

4. Add the chicken breasts to the hot grill pan and cook for 3 to 4 minutes. Rotate the chicken 90 degrees and cook for an additional 3 to 4 minutes, to get crosshatched grill marks. Flip the chicken and repeat on the other side, until the chicken is cooked through, with an internal temperature of 165°F, and has nice grill marks on both sides.

❙ **Per serving** * **Calories:** 410 * **Protein:** 46g * **Carbohydrates:** 6g * **Fat:** 22g

To be honest, a lot of my recipe inspiration comes from the meals I crave from different restaurants. When I was doing the keto diet, one of my favorite restaurants was Olive Garden because you could swap the pasta for broccoli in any dish for a delicious, super-low-carb dinner.

This is the meal I turn to when I want an easy, high-protein comfort food. Besides the sauce, it's all cooked on a single sheet pan, making it low-maintenance and still super satisfying.

The homemade Alfredo sauce is pretty simple, with a base of blended cottage cheese and chicken broth; this gives it that signature creaminess without a ton of fat. But if you're short on time (or energy), your favorite store-bought Alfredo sauce will also work here for a quick, lower-effort dinner.

sheet-pan chicken alfredo with roasted broccoli

2 (6-ounce) boneless, skinless chicken breasts

2 tablespoons extra-virgin olive oil

Kosher salt

Freshly ground black pepper

1 head broccoli, cut into florets

Alfredo Sauce (recipe follows)

1. Preheat the oven to 425°F. Line a sheet pan with parchment paper.

2. Place the chicken breasts on the prepared sheet pan. Drizzle with just enough olive oil to coat, and season generously with salt and pepper on both sides. On the same sheet pan, add the broccoli florets. Drizzle with the remaining olive oil and season with salt and pepper. Toss to combine, then spread it back out into one even layer.

3. Roast the chicken and broccoli until the chicken is cooked through (with an internal temperature of 165°F) and the broccoli is tender and slightly browned around the edges, 20 to 25 minutes.

4. Meanwhile, make the Alfredo Sauce.

5. Remove the chicken and broccoli from the oven. Once the chicken is cool enough to handle, slice it into thin strips or bite-size pieces.

6. To serve, arrange the roasted broccoli on plates or in bowls. Top with the sliced chicken. Drizzle about ½ cup of the Alfredo Sauce over each serving of chicken and broccoli.

(recipe continues)

Makes 4 servings ✳ **Total time:** about 35 minutes
Per serving ✳ **Calories:** 420 ✳ **Protein:** 37g ✳ **Carbohydrates:** 16g ✳ **Fat:** 24g

Alfredo Sauce * Makes 2 cups (4 servings)

2 cups whole-milk
cottage cheese

¼ cup chicken broth

2 tablespoons
unsalted butter

2 garlic cloves, minced

½ cup grated
Parmesan cheese

1 tablespoon heavy
whipping cream

1 teaspoon garlic salt

½ teaspoon freshly
ground black pepper

1. In a blender, combine the cottage cheese and chicken broth and blend until smooth. Set aside.

2. In a large skillet or saucepan, melt the butter over medium heat. Add the garlic and cook until fragrant, 1 to 2 minutes.

3. Remove from the heat and add in the cottage cheese–chicken broth mixture. Stir constantly until the mixture is fully incorporated.

4. Return the pan to low heat and add in the Parmesan, heavy cream, garlic salt, and pepper. Stir constantly until the sauce is smooth and heated through, about 3 minutes. Remove from the heat.

Per serving * **Calories:** 220 * **Protein:** 16g * **Carbohydrates:** 6g * **Fat:** 15g

When I was in high school, all of my friends were obsessed with this chicken teriyaki place at the mall food court. Once I tried it, I realized why it always had the longest line.

I get why teriyaki chicken is a popular mall food—it's honestly a great on-the-go option. It's loaded with protein, usually comes with lots of sautéed veggies, and its sweet-and-savory flavor always hits the spot. And it's also a major part of my home cooking rotation, especially during summer when I can grill the chicken outdoors.

The main driver of the marinade in this recipe is coconut aminos, often used as a gluten-free substitute for soy sauce. It's not as salty, and I think it has a milder, sweeter flavor, so I prefer it over soy sauce for this recipe. I find that the sugar in coconut aminos gives the chicken a lovely, bubbly char, but if you have soy sauce on hand, it will work fine, too.

teriyaki grilled chicken

½ cup coconut aminos

2 tablespoons honey

2 teaspoons minced garlic

½ teaspoon toasted sesame oil

2 pounds boneless, skinless chicken thighs (about 8 thighs)

Kosher salt

Freshly ground black pepper

Neutral oil, for grill

For Serving
Sesame seeds

Green onions, thinly sliced

serving suggestion ⭑ Pair with a freezer bag of stir-fried vegetables, broccoli, and rice for a quick meal. If making broccoli, you can cook it alongside the chicken in a grill basket.

1. **Make the marinade:** In a bowl, whisk together the coconut aminos, honey, garlic, and sesame oil.

2. Place the chicken thighs in a resealable ziplock bag. Pour the marinade over the chicken. Marinate in the fridge for at least 4 hours, or up to overnight.

3. Preheat your grill to medium-high heat and oil the grates.

4. Remove the chicken from the marinade. Reserve ¼ cup of marinade for basting the chicken and set aside (you can discard the rest). Season the chicken all over with salt and pepper.

5. Place the chicken thighs on the grill. Cover and cook for 6 to 7 minutes; then, using a heatproof brush, baste the chicken with some of the reserved marinade. Flip the chicken thighs and baste with the remaining marinade. Cover and continue grilling for 6 to 7 more minutes, until the internal temperature reaches 175°F.

6. Remove the thighs from the grill and serve hot, garnished with sesame seeds and green onions.

tip: And if you plan ahead and marinate the chicken breasts early in the day or the night before, you'll have a meal in around 30 minutes.

Makes 6 servings ⭑ **Total time:** about 30 minutes, plus 4 hours marinating time
Per serving ⭑ **Calories:** 240 ⭑ **Protein:** 26g ⭑ **Carbohydrates:** 13g ⭑ **Fat:** 9g

This is the meal I make when I honestly don't want to cook, but I know I have it in me to just slice up some bell peppers, season some chicken, and throw it all in the oven. Once that part's done, making the green chile crema is a breeze. You don't even need to chop the cilantro.

sheet-pan fajitas
with green chile crema

4 teaspoons ancho chile powder

2 teaspoons kosher salt

2 bell peppers (any color), thinly sliced

1 yellow onion, sliced

2 pounds boneless, skinless chicken thighs

1 tablespoon extra-virgin olive oil

Green Chile Crema

1 cup whole-milk Greek yogurt

Juice of ½ lime

½ cup cilantro leaves

1 (4-ounce) can diced green chiles, drained

¼ teaspoon kosher salt

For Serving

6 (10-inch) low-carb flour tortillas, warmed

Chopped fresh cilantro, for garnish (optional)

1. Preheat the oven to 400°F. Line a sheet pan with parchment paper.

2. Make the ancho seasoning: In a small bowl, stir together the chile powder and salt.

3. Place the bell peppers and onions on the prepared sheet pan, creating a bed for the chicken. Season the bell peppers and onions with half of the ancho seasoning.

4. Coat the chicken thighs with the olive oil and sprinkle both sides with the remaining ancho seasoning. Arrange the seasoned chicken thighs on top of the onions and peppers.

5. Bake in the oven until the veggies are tender and the chicken is cooked through, about 30 minutes.

6. Meanwhile, make the green chile crema: In a blender, combine the yogurt, lime juice, cilantro, diced chiles, and salt and blend until smooth.

7. Once the chicken is cooked, set the oven to broil for about 1 minute, just until the chicken is lightly charred on top.

8. Remove the chicken thighs from the oven and let them rest for a few minutes. Slice the chicken thighs in thin strips against the grain. Serve the chicken with tortillas, and serve the green chile crema for dipping or to drizzle on each fajita. Top with some cilantro, if desired.

serving suggestion *
Serve with tortillas as suggested, or in a bowl with grains and vegetables, or over salad greens.

Makes 6 servings * Total time: about 45 minutes
Per serving * Calories: 340 * Protein: 36g * Carbohydrates: 22g * Fat: 16g

This recipe has all the same flavors as Buffalo chicken dip, but instead of eating it with chips, you fill a wrap and toast it crisp in a skillet. This is another one of those meals I make when I really am not up for a challenge. I know I'll have lunch on the table within half an hour.

I'm partial to Frank's RedHot, but you can use any similar vinegar-based hot sauce. I like to use lavash wraps for this recipe, but any wrap or tortilla you like will work. And of course, plenty of people aren't so keen on blue cheese, and I get that it's not for everyone—if that's you, just replace the blue cheese with more mozzarella or cheddar Jack. For me, the mozzarella and puréed cottage cheese mellow out the pungency of the blue cheese—plus, you get more protein.

buffalo chicken flatbreads

½ cup Frank's RedHot sauce

½ cup whole-milk cottage cheese, puréed until smooth

1 teaspoon ranch seasoning

¼ cup crumbled blue cheese

4 green onions, green tops only, minced

8 ounces cooked chicken breast, shredded (see Tip)

½ cup shredded mozzarella cheese

2 lavash bread wraps or low-carb tortillas

2 teaspoons unsalted butter

1. In a large bowl, combine the hot sauce, puréed cottage cheese, ranch seasoning, blue cheese, and green onions. Add the shredded chicken and toss to coat.

2. Spread half of the Buffalo chicken mixture and ¼ cup of mozzarella in an even layer on top of each wrap or tortilla, covering half of each wrap. Fold the wraps closed to cover the filling.

3. Set a large skillet over medium heat and add the butter. Once the butter is melted, place the wraps in the skillet and cook until golden brown and crispy on both sides, 3 to 4 minutes per side.

4. Remove the wraps from the skillet. Once cool enough to handle, cut them into halves or quarters and serve hot.

tip: It's definitely okay to use store-bought chicken for this recipe. Store-bought rotisserie chicken works best, but in a pinch, even canned chicken will get the job done. It's easy, it's often pre-shredded, and it goes great with the other ingredients in this recipe. If you want to cook the chicken at home, oven-roast two 6-ounce chicken breasts on a sheet pan, seasoned with salt, pepper, and a dash of olive oil. Bake at 375°F for 20 to 25 minutes, or until they reach an internal temperature of at least 165°F. Let cool for 5 minutes and then finely shred with two forks.

Makes 2 servings * **Total time:** about 20 minutes (if starting with cooked chicken)
Per serving * **Calories:** 620 * **Protein:** 61g * **Carbohydrates:** 24g * **Fat:** 35g

fan favorite!

As I've mentioned, one of my first (and favorite) jobs was at a pizza place. They had an incredible Greek salad, and once I learned how to make it, it became a staple recipe for me, especially during high school when I was just learning how to cook.

To me, this salad screams summer, but is delicious year-round if you use cherry tomatoes, which still have a ton of flavor even when they're not in season. A classic Greek salad is made with cucumber, tomatoes, olives, and feta—no lettuce—but you can add lettuce for volume, plus a little extra fiber and crunch.

If you are pressed for time, you can use the breast meat of a store-bought rotisserie chicken (about 2 cups' worth once shredded). You can also chop the vegetables beforehand, make the vinaigrette ahead of time, and mix everything together just before serving.

greek salad with chicken

Pesto-Balsamic
Chicken (page 71)

½ cup Zesty Pepperoncini
Vinaigrette (recipe follows)

10 ounces cherry
tomatoes, halved

12 ounces mini
cucumbers, diced

1 cup diced red onion

Kosher salt

1 cup pitted
Kalamata olives

4 ounces crumbled feta

½ cup finely diced
pepperoncini

tip: To meal prep this, pour 2 tablespoons of the vinaigrette into each bottom of four 20-ounce mason jars. Add tomatoes, cucumbers, onion, olives, feta, and pepperoncini to each jar and season with salt to taste. Top each jar with roughly 3 ounces of chicken. To serve, shake the jar to toss the salad; then pour the contents into a bowl.

1. Prepare the Pesto-Balsamic Chicken. When cool enough to handle, cut the chicken into bite-size pieces and set aside.

2. Make the Zesty Pepperoncini Vinaigrette.

3. Combine the tomatoes, cucumbers, and onion and season with salt to taste. Add the olives, feta, and pepperoncini. Dress with ½ cup of the Zesty Pepperoncini Vinaigrette. Top with the chicken and serve.

Makes 4 servings * **Total time:** about 30 minutes, plus 30 minutes marinating time
Per serving * **Calories:** 640 * **Protein:** 53g * **Carbohydrates:** 21g * **Fat:** 39g

Zesty Pepperoncini Vinaigrette * Makes a generous 1 cup (8 servings)

½ cup extra-virgin olive oil

¼ cup red wine vinegar

Juice of ½ lemon

2 tablespoons
pepperoncini brine

1 teaspoon Dijon mustard

2 tablespoons maple syrup

1 garlic clove, grated

1 teaspoon dried oregano

½ teaspoon kosher salt

¼ teaspoon freshly
ground black pepper

In a small bowl, combine the olive oil, red wine vinegar, lemon juice, pepperoncini brine, Dijon mustard, maple syrup, garlic, oregano, salt, and pepper. Whisk until well combined.

Per 2 tablespoons * **Calories:** 120 * **Protein:** 0g * **Carbohydrates:** 4g * **Fat:** 12g

One of my staples was a frozen bag of blackened chicken tenders they had at Target. They were kind of expensive, so I started working on a recipe. The key to blackening the tenders is the little bit of sweetener in the rub (plus plenty of spices).

Honey mustard is my personal favorite dipping sauce, but these tenders are also great with my Restaurant-Style Ranch Dressing (page 95).

air-fryer blackened chicken tenders
with honey mustard sauce

Honey Mustard Sauce

2 tablespoons Dijon mustard

1 tablespoon yellow mustard

¼ cup light mayonnaise

1 tablespoon sugar-free maple syrup

1 tablespoon honey

Chicken Tenders

1 pound boneless, skinless chicken breasts

1 teaspoon smoked paprika

1 teaspoon Swerve brown sugar erythritol

1 teaspoon kosher salt

½ teaspoon garlic powder

½ teaspoon onion powder

½ teaspoon Cajun seasoning

¼ teaspoon ground thyme

½ teaspoon dry ground mustard

½ teaspoon dried parsley

¼ teaspoon cayenne

1 tablespoon extra-virgin olive oil

1. **Make the honey mustard sauce:** In a small bowl, combine the Dijon mustard, yellow mustard, mayo, syrup, and honey.

2. Preheat the air fryer to 400°F for about 5 minutes.

3. **Prepare the chicken tenders:** Cut each chicken breast into long, thin strips (about 1 inch wide each).

4. **Make the blackened seasoning:** In a bowl or shallow dish, mix together the smoked paprika, Swerve, salt, garlic powder, onion powder, Cajun seasoning, thyme, dry ground mustard, parsley, and cayenne.

5. Pat the chicken tenders dry with paper towels. Then cover them with the olive oil and dip them in the blackened seasoning to ensure they are coated on all sides. Press the spices into the meat to ensure it sticks.

6. Arrange the seasoned chicken tenders in a single layer in the air-fryer basket, making sure they are not overcrowded. You may need to work in batches, depending on the size of your air fryer.

7. Air-fry the chicken tenders until cooked through, 12 to 14 minutes, flipping halfway through.

8. Once the chicken tenders are cooked, remove them from the air fryer and let them rest for a few minutes. Serve them hot, with honey mustard sauce on the side.

Makes 2 servings * Total time: about 20 minutes
Per serving * Calories: 390 * **Protein:** 47g * **Carbohydrates:** 13g * **Fat:** 16g

Elote, or Mexican street corn, is corn on the cob brushed with melted butter, lime juice, mayonnaise, a generous sprinkle of cotija cheese, and a dusting of chili powder and usually served on a skewer. It's one of the best things ever, and if you ever come across a street cart vendor selling it, you have to give it a try.

I still remember when I first tried elote in high school. Back then, I couldn't get past the mayo. But now, with a more seasoned palate and greater appreciation for flavor, I totally get the hype. I was inspired to create this easy air-fryer recipe using the same flavor combo, but replacing the corn with chicken to create the ultimate, high-protein skewer.

elote-style air-fryer chicken skewers

2 pounds boneless, skinless chicken thighs, cut into bite-size pieces

1 tablespoon extra-virgin olive oil

2 teaspoons chile-lime seasoning (such as Tajín or Simply Organic), plus more for garnish

¼ cup light mayonnaise

½ cup grated Cotija or Parmesan cheese

1. In a large bowl, toss the chicken with the olive oil and chile-lime seasoning.

2. If using wooden skewers, soak them in water for at least 30 minutes to prevent burning.

3. Thread the chicken pieces onto 6 skewers, leaving space between the pieces to ensure even cooking.

4. Preheat the air fryer to 375°F for about 5 minutes.

5. Place the chicken skewers in a single layer in the air-fryer basket. You may need to work in batches depending on the size of your air fryer.

6. Air-fry the skewers until the chicken is cooked through, 12 to 15 minutes, flipping halfway through (it should reach an internal temperature of at least 165°F.)

7. While the chicken skewers are still hot, gently brush them with mayonnaise on both sides. Sprinkle with cheese and additional chile-lime seasoning and serve immediately.

Makes 4 servings * **Total time:** about 30 minutes
Per skewer * **Calories:** 270 * **Protein:** 28g * **Carbohydrates:** 1g * **Fat:** 16g

This is another recipe that had the internet in shambles—and understandably so. This pizza takes the meaning of "meat lovers' pizza" to a new level by using a crust made out of ground chicken, cottage cheese, and egg, creating the ultimate high-protein base for your favorite toppings. Here, I'm taking it in a BBQ direction with bacon and red onions, but there are so many ways to make this pizza your own. Make a version using Buffalo sauce instead of BBQ as the base, or try using Alfredo Sauce (page 74) for a creamy, protein-packed mash-up. Whichever way you choose, this pizza is a game-changer.

fan favorite!

bbq "chicken crust" pizza

1 pound ground chicken

½ cup whole-milk cottage cheese

1 large egg

¼ cup grated Parmesan cheese

1 teaspoon Italian seasoning

1 teaspoon kosher salt

Freshly ground black pepper

½ cup sugar-free BBQ sauce

¾ cup shredded mozzarella cheese

¼ cup thinly sliced red onion

¼ cup center cut bacon, cooked, then crumbled

1. Preheat the oven to 400°F. Line a sheet pan with parchment paper.

2. In a large bowl, combine the ground chicken, cottage cheese, egg, Parmesan, Italian seasoning, salt, and pepper. Mix well until combined.

3. Spread the chicken "crust" mixture onto the lined sheet pan, forming it into an even layer about ¼ inch thick. Bake until the crust is firm and golden brown, about 30 minutes.

4. Remove the crust from the oven and spread the BBQ sauce in an even layer over the crust. Sprinkle with the mozzarella and top with the red onion and crumbled bacon.

5. Return the pizza to the oven and bake until the cheese is melted, about 10 minutes.

6. Let the pizza cool for a few minutes before slicing and serving.

Makes 2 servings ★ Total time: about 45 minutes
Per serving ★ Calories: 550 ★ Protein: 75g ★ Carbohydrates: 17g ★ Fat: 22g

Chinese takeout is one of my favorite things to eat. It's nostalgic for me—my family used to order it often when I was growing up—and it's something I haven't mastered cooking on my own. Dumplings are a particular favorite; I love pretty much any kind. And while I haven't learned how to make them well enough to share my own recipe, I have experimented with using the flavors in different applications.

That's where this recipe comes in. I think these dumpling-inspired meatballs capture a lot of the delicious flavors of my favorite dumplings, just without the wonton wrapper. I like to make these in an air fryer, but you can also sear them in a skillet with a bit of oil.

air-fryer chicken dumpling meatballs

Meatballs

1 pound ground chicken

¼ cup panko breadcrumbs

¼ cup coconut aminos

2 large eggs, lightly beaten

¾ cup finely chopped green onions

2 teaspoons minced fresh ginger

4 garlic cloves, minced

1 teaspoon garlic chili oil

1 teaspoon kosher salt

Olive oil cooking spray

Dipping Sauce

3 tablespoons soy sauce

1 tablespoon seasoned rice vinegar

1 teaspoon toasted sesame oil

½ teaspoon chili garlic sauce

For Serving

Thinly sliced green onion

Sesame seeds

1. Make the meatballs: In a large bowl, combine the ground chicken, panko, coconut aminos, eggs, green onions, ginger, garlic, chili oil, and salt. Mix with clean hands until well combined.

2. Shape the mixture into meatballs, about 1 inch in diameter.

3. Preheat the air fryer to 400°F for about 5 minutes. Once preheated, coat the air-fryer basket with cooking spray.

4. Transfer the meatballs to the air fryer in a single layer (you'll need to work in batches). Air-fry each batch for about 10 minutes, or until the meatballs are browned and the inside is cooked through (with an internal temperature of 160°F).

5. Make the dipping sauce: In a small bowl, whisk together the soy sauce, rice vinegar, sesame oil, and chili garlic sauce.

6. Transfer the meatballs to a serving dish. Garnish with green onions and sesame seeds. Serve with the dipping sauce on the side for dipping.

serving suggestion * Serve in a bowl with some roasted broccoli and rice.

Makes 2 servings * **Total time:** about 45 minutes
Per serving * **Calories:** 480 * **Protein:** 61g * **Carbohydrates:** 29g * **Fat:** 11g

This recipe makes use of some of my favorite shortcuts. I use store-bought rotisserie chicken (though if you want to roast chicken at home, feel free). I'm sure a homemade enchilada sauce would be out of this world, but in this case, the canned stuff totally gets the job done (Old El Paso, Las Palmas, and El Pato are my favorite brands). This recipe uses Hidden Valley's Fiesta Ranch Dips Mix, but if you can't find that, substitute a homemade or pre-made taco seasoning.

chicken enchiladas verdes

1 pound store-bought rotisserie chicken meat, shredded

1 cup ⅓ less fat cream cheese, at room temperature

1 (4-ounce) can diced green chiles, drained

1 tablespoon plus 1 teaspoon Hidden Valley Fiesta Ranch Dips Mix

12 corn tortillas

1 (15-ounce) can green enchilada sauce

1 cup shredded mozzarella cheese

For Serving

Pico de gallo

Whole-milk Greek yogurt or sour cream

Shredded iceberg lettuce

tip: Enchiladas are a great meal prep option because they reheat wonderfully, and they taste just as good or even better after a couple days. I mean really, when don't enchiladas sound good?

1. Preheat the oven to 400°F.

2. In a large bowl, combine the chicken, cream cheese, green chiles, and Ranch mix. Toss until the chicken is thoroughly coated and the mixture is fully incorporated.

3. Wrap the tortillas in a damp paper towel and microwave for 2 minutes, flipping once halfway through, until they are soft and pliable.

4. Pour a thin layer of enchilada sauce to cover the bottom of a 9 by 13-inch baking dish. Then, assemble the enchiladas: Fill a tortilla with ¼ cup of the chicken mixture, then roll it up tightly. Place the enchilada seam-side down in the baking dish. Repeat with remaining tortillas and chicken mixture, and line up the enchiladas snugly in the dish.

5. Pour the remaining enchilada sauce on the top of the enchiladas and use a spatula or the back of a spoon to spread it in an even layer. Top with the shredded mozzarella.

6. Cover the baking dish with aluminum foil, transfer to the oven, and bake for 20 minutes. Then remove the foil and continue baking until the cheese is melted and bubbling on top, about 10 more minutes.

7. Let the enchiladas cool slightly before using a metal spatula to serve. Top with pico de gallo, a dollop of Greek yogurt, and a handful of shredded lettuce and serve hot.

Makes 6 servings ✴ **Total time:** about 50 minutes
Per serving ✴ **Calories:** 440 ✴ **Protein:** 29g ✴ **Carbohydrates:** 33g ✴ **Fat:** 20g

One of my favorite high-protein, on-the-go options is Chick-fil-A. They have lots of great items on the menu, but my personal pick is their grilled chicken nuggets, which have just a hint of dill flavor. They're surprisingly easy to recreate at home—no grill needed—and happen to provide the perfect way to use leftover pickle brine. Just an hour of brining does the trick, and honestly, I think this homemade version tastes even better than the original! The ranch is a must-have for dipping, and it's the only ranch recipe you'll ever need—just make sure you buy a ranch seasoning packet that says "restaurant style" for that perfect taste.

air-fryer "grilled" nuggets with ranch

1 pound boneless, skinless chicken thighs, cut into bite-size pieces

1 cup pickle brine

¼ teaspoon baking powder

½ teaspoon kosher salt

¼ teaspoon freshly ground black pepper

Restaurant-Style Ranch Dressing, for serving (recipe follows)

1. Place the bite-size chicken pieces in a large resealable ziplock bag or bowl. Pour the brine from a pickle jar over the chicken, ensuring all pieces are submerged. Seal the bag (or cover the bowl) and transfer to the fridge to marinate for 1 hour.

2. Meanwhile, make the Restaurant-Style Ranch Dressing as directed. Keep refrigerated until ready to serve.

3. When ready to cook, preheat the air fryer to 400°F for a few minutes.

4. Drain the pickle juice from the chicken and pat dry with paper towels. Transfer the chicken to a clean bowl and add the baking powder, salt, and pepper. Toss until the chicken is thoroughly coated.

5. Arrange the chicken pieces in a single layer in the air-fryer basket. Air-fry the chicken until it is crispy and golden brown, 10 to 12 minutes, shaking the basket halfway through to ensure even cooking.

6. Serve the chicken with the Restaurant-Style Ranch Dressing on the side for dipping.

serving suggestion ✶
Pair with waffle fries or roasted potatoes for the complete Chick-fil-A dupe experience. Or, cut up the nuggets and add them to a salad or wrap.

Makes 2 servings ✶ **Total time:** about 30 minutes, plus 1 hour marinating time
Per serving ✶ **Calories:** 300 ✶ **Protein:** 39g ✶ **Carbohydrates:** 4g ✶ **Fat:** 13g

Restaurant-Style Ranch Dressing * Makes about ¾ cup (6 servings)

1 packet ranch seasoning
(I like Hidden Valley
Restaurant-Style
dressing mix)

1 cup whole-milk
Greek yogurt

½ cup whole milk

Pinch freshly ground
black pepper

In a small bowl, combine the ranch seasoning, yogurt, milk, and pepper. Whisk until well combined. Cover and refrigerate until ready to serve.

❚ Per 2 tablespoons * Calories: 25 * Protein: 2g * Carbohydrates: 1g * Fat: 1g

You've heard of a lettuce wrap—so why can't a bell pepper act as a slice of bread? I'm asking because this bell pepper "sandwich" with deli turkey and bacon became one of my most viral recipe videos. (Social media is funny that way . . . you just never know what's going to resonate.) But to me, it just makes sense. Using the bell pepper as the "bread" makes this a wonderful summertime recipe—it's crunchy, refreshing, and low-carb. Plus, the bacon goes so well with the pepper, and the cream cheese and turkey really make for a satiating meal. A sprinkle of everything bagel seasoning brings a pop of flavor.

bell pepper turkey & bacon "sandwiches"

2 large red bell peppers

¼ cup cream cheese

Everything bagel seasoning, to taste

8 slices deli turkey

4 slices center cut bacon, fully cooked and cut in half

¼ red onion, thinly sliced

8 dill pickle slices

1. Using a sharp knife, cut each bell pepper in half vertically. Remove the seeds and cut out any white membrane.

2. Using the back of a spoon, spread 1 tablespoon of cream cheese around the inside of each bell pepper half. Sprinkle everything bagel seasoning over the cream cheese. On each bell pepper half, layer 2 slices of turkey, 2 pieces of bacon, a few slices of red onion, and 2 pickle slices. (It works better to fill both halves equally, rather than putting all the toppings on one side of the bell pepper.)

3. Place the filled bell pepper halves together to make two sandwiches. With a sharp knife, cut the sandwiches on the diagonal and serve.

tip: Try to find bell peppers that are relatively straight-sided and symmetrical—it'll be easier to turn them into a sandwich. Cut on the diagonal (rather than straight across) for a less-messy "sandwich" bite.

Makes 2 sandwiches ★ Total time: about 5 minutes
Per sandwich ★ Calories: 300 ★ Protein: 18g ★ Carbohydrates: 16g ★ Fat: 19g

These Mediterranean-style meatballs are so easy and flavorful—I can't wait for you to try them. They're flecked with feta, spinach, garlic, and sun-dried tomatoes. I like them best made with ground turkey, but feel free to use a ground meat of your choice. They're also excellent for meal prep: you can make a whole batch, freeze them raw, and cook them a few at a time.

I usually make these in the air fryer, but you could also bake them in the oven (bake at 375°F until almost cooked, and then finish off by broiling them for a minute or by searing them in a hot skillet, just to get some browning). The tzatziki sauce is classic and simple—yogurt, cucumber, garlic, lemon, and olive oil—but if you're short on time, store-bought tzatziki sauce will work just fine.

mediterranean–style meatballs with tzatziki sauce

Tzatziki Sauce

1 medium cucumber

1 cup whole-milk Greek yogurt

2 garlic cloves, minced

1½ teaspoons fresh lemon juice

1 tablespoon extra-virgin olive oil

1 tablespoon chopped fresh dill

Kosher salt

Freshly ground black pepper

1. Make the tzatziki sauce: Grate the cucumber on the large holes of a box grater. Transfer the grated cucumber to a sieve and press out any excess water. In a medium bowl, combine the grated cucumber with the yogurt, garlic, lemon juice, olive oil, and dill and mix until well combined. Season with salt and pepper to taste. Refrigerate for at least 30 minutes before serving.

2. Preheat the air fryer to 375°F for 5 minutes.

3. Make the meatballs: Place the spinach, garlic, and sun-dried tomatoes together on a cutting board and finely chop them (this will ensure that every bite of meatball has a blend of all the ingredients). Crumble the feta on top of the mixture and continue chopping until you have a finely chopped mixture. Transfer the mixture to a large bowl and add the oregano, salt, and pepper. Stir until fully incorporated.

4. Add the egg and breadcrumbs to the bowl and stir until fully incorporated. Add the ground turkey and continue mixing until well combined.

serving suggestion *
Serve over cauliflower or white rice, on a salad, or throw into a wrap or pita for a quick lunch.

| **Makes 4 servings (16 meatballs)** * **Total time:** about 50 minutes
Per serving * **Calories:** 360 * **Protein:** 36g * **Carbohydrates:** 16g * **Fat:** 20g

Meatballs

⅔ cup chopped spinach

2 garlic cloves, minced

¼ cup finely chopped
sun-dried tomatoes
(drained, if oil-packed)

½ cup crumbled feta

1 teaspoon dried oregano

1 teaspoon kosher salt

½ teaspoon freshly
ground black pepper

1 large egg, lightly beaten

¼ cup dried breadcrumbs

1 pound 93% lean
ground turkey

Olive oil cooking spray

5. Using clean, washed hands, divide the turkey mixture into 16 equal portions and shape into 1- to 1½-inch meatballs.

6. Lightly coat the air-fryer basket with cooking spray. Arrange the meatballs in the basket in a single layer (cook in batches if needed).

7. Air-fry the meatballs at 375°F until they are golden brown on the outside and reach an internal temperature of at least 165°F, about 10 minutes per batch.

8. Remove the meatballs from the air fryer and let them rest for a few minutes. Drizzle with the tzatziki sauce and serve hot.

It could just be me, but I feel like a good store-bought turkey or chicken sausage is hard to find. Homemade versions taste so much better, and they're a lot easier to make than you would think. This recipe can be made with ground chicken or turkey, and I think it's the perfect combination of a savory and spicy sausage; I like mine highly seasoned, as you'll see here.

sweet heat breakfast sausage

1 pound ground chicken or turkey

2 tablespoons Swerve brown sugar erythritol

2 tablespoons hot honey

1 teaspoon poultry seasoning

1 teaspoon seasoned salt

½ teaspoon freshly ground black pepper

½ teaspoon ground or rubbed sage

½ teaspoon red pepper flakes

1½ teaspoons extra-virgin olive oil, plus more as needed

1. In a large bowl, combine the chicken or turkey, Swerve, hot honey, poultry seasoning, seasoned salt, black pepper, sage, and red pepper flakes. Mix until well combined.

2. Using clean, washed hands, divide the sausage mixture into 8 equal portions. Form into sausage patties about 4 inches in diameter. (If storing, you can freeze the patties at this point and have them ready for whenever you need them.)

3. To cook the patties, line a plate with paper towels and set it near the stovetop. Set a large skillet or cast-iron pan over medium heat and add the olive oil. Once the skillet is hot, add the sausage patties in a single layer, working in batches to avoid overcrowding the pan. Cook until the patties are well-browned on both sides (2 to 3 minutes per side). Transfer the sausage patties to the paper towels to drain any excess grease. Serve hot.

serving suggestion * I often use these to make Sweet & Spicy Breakfast Sandwiches (page 41), but I also like them served alongside some Jammy Eggs (page 45) for a simple, classic breakfast.

Makes 8 sausage patties * **Total time:** about 15 minutes
Per sausage patty * **Calories:** 80 * **Protein:** 13g * **Carbohydrates:** 8g * **Fat:** 2g

This dish was inspired by the grilled chicken and the corn salsa at Chipotle. It's spicy, but you can easily adjust the spice level to your liking by changing the amount of chipotle peppers in adobo sauce. Funny story: the first time I made this dish, I didn't realize how hot chipotle peppers are, and I used the whole can. Don't make my mistake!

grilled chipotle chicken
with corn salsa

Grilled Chicken

2 to 3 whole chipotle peppers in adobo sauce, plus 2 tablespoons sauce from the can

1 garlic clove, minced

1 tablespoon fresh lime juice

2 tablespoons extra-virgin olive oil

1 teaspoon kosher salt

½ teaspoon freshly ground black pepper

1½ pounds boneless, skinless chicken thighs (about 6 thighs)

Neutral oil, for grill

Corn Salsa

2 cups corn kernels, fresh, grilled, or thawed frozen

¼ cup finely diced red onion

¼ cup chopped fresh cilantro

1 tablespoon fresh lime juice

1 tablespoon fresh lemon juice

1 jalapeño, seeded and finely diced

Kosher salt

Freshly ground black pepper

1. Make the marinade: In a blender or food processor, combine the chipotle peppers, adobo sauce, garlic, lime juice, olive oil, salt, and black pepper. Blend until smooth.

2. Marinate the chicken: Pour the marinade over the chicken thighs in a bowl or resealable ziplock bag. Marinate for at least 30 minutes, or up to overnight for best results.

3. Meanwhile, make the corn salsa: In a medium bowl, toss together the corn, red onion, cilantro, lime juice, lemon juice, and jalapeño. Season with salt and pepper to taste and store in the refrigerator until ready to serve.

4. Preheat a grill to medium-high heat and oil the grates.

5. Remove the chicken from the marinade and allow any excess to drip off. Grill the chicken thighs until nicely charred on both sides, 5 to 7 minutes per side, and the internal temperature reaches 175°F.

6. Let the chicken rest 2 to 3 minutes before serving. Slice or leave whole and serve topped with the corn salsa.

Makes 4 servings * **Total time:** about 35 minutes, plus 30 minutes marinating time
Per serving * **Calories:** 330 * **Protein:** 32g * **Carbohydrates:** 20g * **Fat:** 14g

serving suggestions * You can make this into a bowl and serve it over iceberg lettuce with pico de gallo, guacamole, shredded cheese, and Greek yogurt or sour cream. Or enjoy with a side of fruit topped with lime juice, Tajín, and chamoy. If you're not familiar with the latter two, they're both popular chile lime–based Mexican seasonings, and they add a ton of flavor. They're delicious on fresh fruit on a hot day!

I have always loved miso-glazed salmon and cod, so I decided to try it on chicken, and what do you know, it quickly became one of my favorites. The chicken will come out sweet but still have lots of umami flavor, and because the recipe calls for thighs, the meat will stay very juicy and tender as it cooks.

I've paired miso with sweet potatoes in the past, so I knew this would be the perfect combo for a quick and easy sheet-pan meal. This dish is also an excellent addition to your list of great meal-prep recipes.

miso-maple chicken
with sweet potatoes

3 tablespoons white miso paste

3 tablespoons maple syrup

1½ tablespoons soy sauce

1 tablespoon seasoned rice vinegar

1½ pounds boneless, skinless chicken thighs (about 6 thighs)

2 large sweet potatoes, peeled and cut into ½-inch cubes

1 tablespoon extra-virgin olive oil

Kosher salt

Freshly ground black pepper

1. Preheat the oven to 425°F. Line a sheet pan with parchment paper.

2. Make the miso-maple glaze: In a small bowl, whisk together the miso, maple syrup, soy sauce, and rice vinegar until well combined.

3. Pat the chicken thighs dry and place them on one side of the prepared sheet pan. Brush the thighs generously with the glaze.

4. Toss the sweet potatoes with olive oil and salt and pepper to taste. Spread them out in a single layer on the other side of the sheet pan.

5. Transfer the sheet pan to the oven and roast the chicken and sweet potatoes for 30 minutes, tossing the sweet potatoes and flipping the chicken thighs halfway through.

6. After 30 minutes, set the oven to broil for 1 to 2 minutes to give the chicken thighs a caramelized top. Watch carefully to prevent burning.

7. Remove the pan from the oven and toss the sweet potatoes in the juices on the sheet pan to give them extra flavor. Serve hot.

serving suggestion ✶
Serve this with some quinoa and a green salad for a super satisfying meal.

Makes 4 servings ✶ **Total time:** about 40 minutes
Per serving ✶ **Calories:** 400 ✶ **Protein:** 33g ✶ **Carbohydrates:** 35g ✶ **Fat:** 14g

beef

I love Korean BBQ, and beef bulgogi is my favorite thing to order when I go. It's thinly sliced beef marinated in a mixture of soy sauce, onion, garlic, ginger, Asian pear, and some kind of sweetener, sometimes with gochujang (Korean red pepper paste) added for spice. This is my take on it—I like to serve it wrapped in lettuce leaves. If you have time to marinate the beef overnight, I highly recommend it. It will make the meat so much more flavorful.

spicy bulgogi

¼ cup plus 2 tablespoons coconut aminos or soy sauce

2 teaspoons toasted sesame oil

2 teaspoons garlic chili oil

¼ cup gochujang (see Note)

6 green onions, minced

4 garlic cloves, minced

1 teaspoon minced fresh ginger

2 pounds top sirloin steak, very thinly sliced

For Serving

Butter or romaine lettuce leaves

Sesame seeds

1. Make the marinade: In a medium bowl, whisk together the coconut aminos, 3 tablespoons of water, the sesame oil, garlic chili oil, gochujang, green onions, garlic, and ginger. Whisk until fully incorporated. Add the beef to the bowl with the marinade and toss to coat. Marinate in the fridge for 4 hours, or up to overnight.

2. Set a large skillet over medium-high heat. Add the marinated beef to the skillet in an even layer, covering the surface of the pan. Let the beef cook undisturbed until the marinade starts to evaporate and the beef begins to brown, 5 to 7 minutes. Then use a spatula to break the beef up into smaller pieces, stir, and cook to your preferred doneness.

3. Serve with lettuce leaves to make wraps. Garnish with sesame seeds.

tip: Bulgogi is best made with shaved meat because the thin cut keeps it tender, but that's not always easy to find at the grocery store. When I can't find it, I buy a whole cut of sirloin and freeze it for 45 minutes to 1 hour. Once it is firm enough to slice thin but not rock-solid, I shave it at home using a sharp knife.

note: Gochujang is a popular Korean condiment made primarily of red chili powder and fermented soybeans. It's a little bit sweet, a little bit spicy, and somewhat savory. It adds a great flavor to dishes. You can buy gochujang at most Asian markets, or in the refrigerated or international section of your local grocery store.

serving suggestion *
The classic pairing is white rice, but lower-carb options include cauliflower rice and steamed edamame. Never skip the kimchi!

Makes 6 servings * **Total time:** about 20 minutes, plus 4 hours marinating time
Per serving * **Calories:** 350 * **Protein:** 29g * **Carbohydrates:** 16g * **Fat:** 19g

Growing up, my go-to steak to order at a restaurant was a filet mignon—at the time, I was scared of all the fat that comes on a ribeye or strip steak. Filets are very lean, but they're also incredibly tender. In foodie circles, they get a bad rap because people say they have no flavor compared to fattier cuts. But I disagree; I think they have their own unique lean-meat flavor!

To me, the most important part of a steak is the sear on it, which is why I like to cut the filet mignon into two thin medallions. They take less time to cook, and you get more of that seared crust in every bite. As for the Creole-seasoned blue cheese butter that goes on top, well, even my boyfriend—who insists he hates blue cheese—loves it.

creole blue cheese filet medallions

2 (12 ounce) filet mignon steaks (at least 2 inches thick)

1 teaspoon Creole seasoning

¼ cup blue cheese

2 tablespoons butter, at room temperature

1 tablespoon neutral oil, divided

Kosher salt

Freshly ground black pepper

1. Using a sharp knife, cut the steaks horizontally through the center to create 4 medallions, each roughly 1 inch thick.

2. Make the blue-cheese butter: In a small bowl, mix together the Creole seasoning, blue cheese, and butter. Set aside.

3. Cook the steaks: Coat the medallions with ½ tablespoon of neutral oil and season generously with salt and pepper.

4. Set a large skillet over medium-high heat and add the remaining ½ tablespoon of neutral oil. Once the oil is very hot, almost smoking, add the steak medallions and sear until a crust forms on both sides, 1 to 2 minutes per side. Use a meat press or sturdy metal spatula to ensure a nice crust and even cooking.

5. Remove the medallions from the skillet and transfer to a sheet pan.

6. Set the oven to broil and allow to preheat for 5 to 10 minutes. Top each medallion with equal portions of the blue cheese–butter mixture, then transfer to the oven and broil for 1 to 2 minutes, until the butter mixture is melted and slightly browned.

7. Remove from the oven and serve immediately.

serving suggestion *
This dish pairs great with most starches, including roasted or mashed cauliflower, delicata or butternut squash, or potatoes—mashed potatoes, baked potatoes, roasted sweet potatoes, you name it.

| Makes 4 servings * Total time: about 15 minutes
| Per serving * Calories: 440 * Protein: 35g * Carbohydrates: 0g * Fat: 33g

I always love going to Brazilian steakhouses, where they serve grilled meat by the skewer and a few different sauces to go with. My favorite is the herby, tangy, bright green chimichurri that I now can't live without.

Chimichurri goes great on all cuts of grilled meat, and even though it's simple to prepare (it's basically a garlic-herb vinaigrette), it makes every home-cooked steak feel fancy. I make it at least once a week. For me, the key to a really good chimichurri is to chop up the herbs as finely as possible—once you think you're done chopping, keep going for another minute or so.

As for steak seasonings, my two favorites are Gibsons Steakhouse Seasoning Salt, which I find at Costco or online, and Black & Tan Steak Seasoning from Fire & Smoke Society, which I get at Walmart. Both are great options, but feel free to use your favorite.

grilled flank steak
with chimichurri

Chimichurri

¼ cup finely chopped fresh parsley

2 tablespoons finely chopped fresh oregano

2 garlic cloves, minced

3 tablespoons extra-virgin olive oil

2 tablespoons red wine vinegar

1 teaspoon finely chopped Calabrian chiles in oil

¼ teaspoon kosher salt

¼ teaspoon freshly ground black pepper

Steak

2 pounds flank steak

Neutral oil, for grill

1 tablespoon extra-virgin olive oil

1 tablespoon Gibsons Steakhouse Seasoning Salt

1. Remove the flank steaks from the fridge and allow them to sit at room temperature for 30 minutes before cooking.

2. Meanwhile, make the chimichurri: In a medium bowl, combine the parsley, oregano, and garlic. Add the olive oil, red wine vinegar, Calabrian chiles, salt, and black pepper and stir well to combine. Transfer to the fridge until ready to serve.

3. Preheat the grill to high and oil the grates. Rub the steaks with olive oil and coat with Gibsons Steakhouse Seasoning Salt.

4. Place the steaks on the grill, cover, and cook until they are well browned and start to char, about 5 minutes. Flip and grill for another 5 minutes. Continue cooking to your preferred doneness. (My preference is medium, at 135°F. For medium-rare, remove at 125°F; for medium-well, cook to 145°F.)

5. Remove the steaks from the grill and cover them loosely with foil. Let them rest for 5 minutes before slicing them against the grain into bite-size pieces.

6. Serve the steak hot, topped with chimichurri.

Makes 4 servings * **Total time:** about 30 minutes
Per serving * **Calories:** 320 * **Protein:** 34g * **Carbohydrates:** 1g * **Fat:** 19g

I love to cook pot roast during the cold winter months when I just want to be warm. The broth is rich and creamy, with delicious chuck roast in every bite. Chuck roast is a relatively affordable cut of boneless beef. If you're short on time, you can buy stew beef, which is often just pre-cut bites of chuck roast—they'll cook a little faster.

pot roast with mushroom gravy

½ bunch of fresh rosemary

3 pounds beef chuck roast

2 tablespoons extra-virgin olive oil, divided

Kosher salt

Freshly ground black pepper

8 ounces white mushrooms, sliced

1 large yellow onion, chopped

4 garlic cloves, minced

1 quart beef broth

1 tablespoon soy sauce

1 tablespoon Worcestershire sauce

tip: I make this in my Dutch oven, but it would also work in a slow cooker. To adapt for a slow cooker, simply transfer the seared meat, broth, and sautéed vegetables to the slow cooker instead of placing the dish in the oven. Cook on low for 8 hours, or on high for 4 hours.

serving suggestion ✻
Serve over buttery mashed potatoes or with an oven-warmed baguette, and you have the perfect cozy meal.

1. Preheat the oven to 275°F.

2. Wrap the rosemary with kitchen twine and set aside.

3. Cut the chuck roast into 4 pieces. Coat with 1 tablespoon olive oil and season generously on all sides with salt and pepper.

4. Set a large Dutch oven over medium-high heat and add the remaining olive oil. Once the oil is hot, add the chuck roast and cook until browned on all sides, 4 to 5 minutes per side. Remove the roast from the Dutch oven and set aside on a cutting board.

5. Add the mushrooms to the Dutch oven and cook until most of the moisture is released and the mushrooms begin to brown, about 5 minutes. Add the onion and cook until soft and translucent, about 5 minutes. Add the garlic and cook just until fragrant, stirring often, about 30 seconds.

6. Stir in the broth, soy sauce, and Worcestershire sauce. Return the chuck roast to the Dutch oven, nestling it among the onions and mushrooms. Add the bundle of rosemary and cover the Dutch oven with the lid.

7. Transfer the pot to the oven and cook until the roast is tender and easily shredded with a fork, about 4 hours.

8. Remove the pot from the oven and discard the rosemary bundle. Remove the meat from the Dutch oven and set aside.

9. Using an immersion blender or a regular blender, blend the cooked vegetables into the cooking liquid until you have a smooth, creamy sauce. Season with salt and pepper to taste.

10. Slice or shred the beef and arrange it on a serving platter. Pour the sauce over the beef and serve (though save some for later—it tastes even better as leftovers).

Makes 8 servings ✻ **Total time:** about 4 hours 30 minutes
Per serving ✻ **Calories:** 470 ✻ **Protein:** 47g ✻ **Carbohydrates:** 4g ✻ **Fat:** 29g

If you're looking for a dish to impress, this is it. The sauce is rich and decadent, and the beef is so tender that you can cut it with a spoon. It's an instant classic. Short ribs are incredibly tender when braised, and they come with quite a bit of fat, which means lots of flavor.

Short ribs do run on the pricier side, so if you want a budget-friendly hack, swap them out for a 3-pound chuck roast cut into 6 equal pieces (to sort of resemble short ribs). The meat might not be as melt-in-your-mouth tender, but the flavor will be great.

For me, the umami seasoning blend is the secret ingredient that takes this dish to another level. There are many brands, but I like the ones that have a base of mushroom powder. They're fairly easy to find—Target and Trader Joe's both sell them, and you can find many more options online.

red wine–braised short ribs

6 (6 ounce) bone-in beef short ribs (sometimes labeled "English-style")

2 tablespoons extra-virgin olive oil

1 tablespoon kosher salt

2 teaspoons freshly ground black pepper

1 large yellow onion, chopped

4 garlic cloves, minced

¼ cup tomato paste

1 cup dry red wine

2 cups beef broth

1 tablespoon Worcestershire sauce

2 teaspoons mushroom-based umami seasoning blend

2 sprigs fresh thyme

2 sprigs fresh rosemary

1. Preheat the oven to 275°F.

2. Coat the short ribs with 1 tablespoon of olive oil, and rub with salt and pepper.

3. Set a large Dutch oven over medium-high heat and add the remaining 1 tablespoon of olive oil. Once the oil is hot, add the short ribs and sear until they develop a deep brown crust on all sides, about 5 minutes per side. Remove the short ribs from the Dutch oven and set aside on a cutting board.

4. In the same Dutch oven, add the onion and sauté until softened and translucent, 5 to 7 minutes. Add the garlic and tomato paste and cook for another 3 minutes, stirring frequently to prevent burning. Pour in the red wine to deglaze the pot, using a wooden spoon to scrape up any browned bits from the bottom. Continue cooking until the wine reduces by half, about 5 minutes.

(recipe continues)

Makes 6 servings * **Total time:** about 5 hours
Per serving * **Calories:** 500 * **Protein:** 22g * **Carbohydrates:** 7g * **Fat:** 39g

5. Stir in the beef broth, Worcestershire sauce, and umami seasoning. Return the seared short ribs to the pot, nestling them into the liquid and vegetables. Tie the rosemary and thyme sprigs with kitchen twine to make an herb bundle and add it to the Dutch oven. Bring the mixture to a simmer, then cover with the lid.

6. Transfer the pot to the oven to braise until the meat is fork-tender, about 4 hours.

7. Once the meat is cooked, remove the pot from the oven. Discard the herb bundle and use a large spoon to skim any excess fat off the surface.

8. Serve the short ribs hot, with the braising liquid poured on top.

I feel pretty passionately that I'm a natural at chili. I used to enter it in a local chili cooking competition, and the first year I entered (only my second time ever making chili), it came in second place. And I've only gotten better since.

Chili is one of those dishes that I make a little differently every time, but here are the best tips I have for you before you jump in:

* The key to this chili is seasoning the pot twice: once when you brown the beef and vegetables, and again after you add all the liquids and tomatoes to the pot. This creates multiple layers of flavor.

* I like using chuck roast cut into cubes for big meaty bites, but you can easily substitute ground beef.

* My secret non-negotiable ingredients are beef and chicken bouillon, diced fire-roasted tomatoes, smoked paprika, and very finely chopped bell peppers. I like to use a combination of red, green, and yellow bell peppers, but you can use whatever you prefer.

* Many people add beans to their chili. I'm personally not a fan, but certainly add them if you so choose.

* If you own a smoker, try smoking the chuck roast instead of searing it. Smoke the whole roast at 225°F for 1 to 2 hours, or until it has a nice bark and some of the fat has rendered. Then cut it up and transfer it to the chili to continue to cook for the additional 3 hours.

* If you'd like a lower spice level, swap the jalapeños for a can of mild diced green chiles.

chuck roast chili

Spice Mixture

¼ cup plus 2 tablespoons chili powder

2 tablespoons kosher salt

1 tablespoon garlic powder

1 tablespoon onion powder

1 tablespoon smoked paprika

1 teaspoon freshly ground black pepper

½ teaspoon cayenne pepper

Chili

3 pounds chuck roast, cut into 1-inch chunks

Kosher salt

Freshly ground black pepper

1 tablespoon extra-virgin olive oil

2 bell peppers (multiple colors), diced

1 large yellow onion, finely diced

2 jalapeños, seeded and diced

4 garlic cloves, minced

⅓ cup tomato paste

1 cup beef broth

1 (28-ounce) can diced fire-roasted tomatoes

1 tablespoon dark cocoa powder

2 tablespoons Worcestershire sauce

1 tablespoon apple cider vinegar

1 tablespoon hot sauce of choice

1 teaspoon chicken bouillon paste (or 2 cubes)

1 teaspoon beef bouillon paste (or 2 cubes)

For Serving

Chopped green onions

Sour cream or Greek yogurt

Shredded cheddar cheese

(recipe continues)

Makes 8 servings * Total time: about 3 hours 20 minutes
Per serving * Calories: 510 * Protein: 45g * Carbohydrates: 18g * Fat: 29

1. Preheat the oven to 275°F.

2. **Make the spice mixture:** In a small bowl, stir together the chili powder, salt, garlic powder, onion powder, smoked paprika, black pepper, and cayenne.

3. **Make the chili:** Pat the chuck roast chunks dry with paper towels and season with salt and black pepper.

4. Set a large pot or Dutch oven over medium-high heat and add the olive oil. Once the oil is hot, add the chuck roast to the Dutch oven and sear on all sides until well browned, about 15 minutes. Remove the meat and set aside on a cutting board.

5. To the same pot, add the bell peppers and onion. Sauté until the bell peppers are softened and the onion is translucent, about 5 minutes. Add the jalapeños and garlic and cook for about 1 minute, or until the garlic is fragrant. Add the tomato paste and half of the spice mixture and stir to incorporate. Continue to sauté for 2 minutes.

6. Return the seared chuck roast to the pot. Add the beef broth, tomatoes, cocoa powder, Worcestershire sauce, apple cider vinegar, hot sauce, chicken and beef bouillon, and the remaining spice mixture. Stir well to ensure all the ingredients are incorporated.

7. Bring the mixture to a simmer, then cover with a lid and transfer to the oven to cook until the meat is tender, about 3 hours.

8. Serve hot, topped with green onions, sour cream, and cheddar cheese to taste.

To this day, these Air-Fryer Garlic Butter Steak Bites remain one of my most viral, popular recipes. When I came up with it, I had tried to use the air fryer to cook steak a few times, but I wasn't a huge fan. I figured out that the trick is to cut the steak into bite-size pieces and make sure every piece is well-seasoned, so they get a flavorful crust but are tender on the inside.

This recipe calls for marinating the steak in Worcestershire sauce, which gives the crust great flavor. Then, once they're cooked, they're tossed in a simple but rich garlic butter. Super easy, super delicious. I use sirloin for this, but a filet or ribeye would work well, too.

air-fryer garlic butter steak bites

1 pound sirloin steak, cut into bite-size pieces

1 tablespoon Worcestershire sauce

1 teaspoon extra-virgin olive oil

½ tablespoon steak seasoning

3 tablespoons unsalted butter

3 garlic cloves, minced

1 tablespoon minced fresh chives

1. Place the steak pieces in a bowl. Add the Worcestershire sauce and olive oil. Mix well to coat the steak evenly. Marinate in the fridge for 30 minutes.

2. Preheat the air fryer to 425°F (or highest heat setting) for about 5 minutes.

3. Drip off any excess marinade and season the steak with the steak seasoning. Place the steak bites in a single layer in the air-fryer basket. Cook in batches if needed. Air-fry the steak for 8 to 10 minutes, shaking the basket halfway through.

4. While the steak bites are cooking, make the garlic butter: In a small saucepan, melt the butter over medium heat. Add the garlic and sauté for about 1 minute, until fragrant. Remove from the heat.

5. Once the steak is done, transfer to a medium bowl. Pour the garlic butter over the steak bites, sprinkle with the chives, and toss to coat evenly.

serving suggestion *
Serve with Garlic Cauliflower Mash (page 232) or Honey Butter–Glazed Carrots (page 240).

Makes 4 servings * Total time: about 45 minutes
Per serving * Calories: 300 * Protein: 21g * Carbohydrates: 2g * Fat: 24g

Every St. Patrick's Day when I was younger, my mom would pull out the slow cooker to make corned beef with cabbage. My brothers weren't huge fans, but I loved it. I always looked forward to one day carrying on the tradition myself—and I haven't missed a year yet.

Corned beef brisket has two cuts: point and flat. Both work well, but I prefer the point cut for its extra fat, which adds great flavor. Typically, corned beef is served with a horseradish or mustard sauce; adding honey mustard was my own twist. I like the nice crust it creates on top, and you can make extra to use as a dip on the side. (You can easily swap the honey for maple syrup or sugar-free maple syrup.)

slow-cooker honey mustard corned beef & cabbage

1 large yellow onion, chopped

3 large carrots, peeled and cut into large pieces

4 pounds point cut corned beef brisket (with spice packet)

1 quart beef broth

¼ cup honey

2 tablespoons Dijon mustard

2 tablespoons whole-grain mustard

Pinch cayenne pepper

1 small head cabbage, cut into chunks

serving suggestion * For leftovers, turn this recipe into Reuben sandwiches the next day—toast rye bread with Thousand Island dressing, then add a generous layer of corned beef, Swiss cheese, and sauerkraut.

1. In a slow cooker, combine the onion and carrots. Set the corned beef brisket on top of the vegetables, fat-side down. Sprinkle the included spice packet over the brisket. Pour the beef broth around the brisket. Cover and cook on high for 3 hours.

2. Meanwhile make the honey mustard mixture: In a small bowl, combine the honey, Dijon mustard, whole-grain mustard, and cayenne. Mix well and refrigerate until needed.

3. After 3 hours, flip the brisket so it's fat-side up. Coat the top of the brisket with the honey mustard mixture. Cover and continue cooking on high for another 2 hours.

4. Add the cabbage to the crockpot. Continue cooking on low until the cabbage is tender and the brisket is easily shredded with a fork, about 1 hour.

5. Remove the brisket from the slow cooker and let it rest for a few minutes before cutting against the grain into thin slices.

6. Serve the corned beef with the stewed onions, carrots, and cabbage on the side.

Makes 12 servings * **Total time:** about 8 hours 30 minutes
Per serving * **Calories:** 340 * **Protein:** 25g * **Carbohydrates:** 13g * **Fat:** 12g

It's no secret that most of the recipes I make come from takeout cravings. This one is inspired by the steak at Chipotle. Marinated with chipotle chile and garlic, then cooked to perfection on a grill, it's packed with smoky, bold flavor. I'm using top sirloin here—a cut that doesn't get as much attention as ribeye or flank, but has a great balance of flavor and a bit of marbling that's perfect for grilling.

The fajita sauce is made with two staples I always keep in the fridge: super-hot salsa and Greek yogurt or sour cream, creating the ultimate balance of heat and creaminess.

chipotle-inspired grilled steak fajitas

Marinated Steak

3 whole chipotle peppers in adobo sauce, plus 3 tablespoons sauce from can

2 garlic cloves, minced

¼ teaspoon ground cumin

¼ cup extra-virgin olive oil

1 teaspoon kosher salt

½ teaspoon freshly ground black pepper

1½ pounds top sirloin steak

Neutral oil, for grill

Fajita Veggies

1 red bell pepper, sliced

1 green bell pepper, sliced

1 large onion, sliced

1 teaspoon extra-virgin olive oil

1 teaspoon balsamic vinegar

½ teaspoon ancho chile powder

½ teaspoon kosher salt

Freshly ground black pepper

For Serving

¼ cup store-bought hot red salsa

½ cup whole-milk Greek yogurt or sour cream

6 (10-inch) low-carb flour tortillas, warmed

1. Make the marinade: In a blender, combine the chipotle peppers, adobo sauce, garlic, cumin, olive oil, salt, and pepper and blend until smooth.

2. Marinate the steak: Place the steak in a resealable ziplock bag or shallow dish and pour the chipotle marinade over the steak. Seal the bag or cover the dish and refrigerate for at least 30 minutes, or up to overnight.

(recipe continues)

Makes 6 servings * **Total time:** about 40 minutes, plus 30 minutes marinating time
Per serving * **Calories:** 390 * **Protein:** 32g * **Carbohydrates:** 23g * **Fat:** 22g

3. Make the fajita veggies: Line a sheet pan with parchment paper. In a large bowl, toss together the bell peppers, onion, olive oil, balsamic vinegar, chile powder, and salt, and season with black pepper to taste. Spread the veggies in a single layer on the prepared sheet pan.

4. Preheat the grill to high and oil the grates.

5. Once the grill is hot, place the sheet pan of veggies on the grill and close the lid. Roast until the veggies are tender and caramelized, about 15 minutes, stirring halfway through. Remove the sheet pan from the grill and set aside.

6. Remove the steak from the marinade and let any excess marinade drip off. Grill the steak to your desired level of doneness, 5 to 7 minutes per side (with an internal temperature of 130°F for medium-rare, or 135°F for medium).

7. Remove the steak from the grill and let it rest for 5 minutes before slicing it against the grain into thin strips.

8. To serve: In a small bowl, whisk together the hot salsa and yogurt to create the sauce. Add a generous portion of caramelized fajita veggies and sliced sirloin to each warmed tortilla. Top with the yogurt sauce and serve hot.

I love burgers so much! But can we normalize ditching the burger bun? What if I took all the flavors I love in burgers and put it in . . . a . . . bowl . . . ?

I was inspired by In-N-Out Burger and their classic bun-free secret menu item, the Flying Dutchman. It's simply a burger patty with cheese, often ordered with grilled onions on top. This dish is my easy at-home version.

I like to serve my "Flying Dutchman" on a bed of crisp greens, almost akin to a burger lettuce wrap. But my favorite part of this recipe is the burger sauce: it adds a little bit of a sweetness and cuts the richness from the combination of the burger, cheese, and onions.

caramelized onion burger bowls

Special Sauce

¼ cup light mayonnaise

2 teaspoons ketchup

1 tablespoon pickle brine

2 teaspoons relish

2 teaspoons yellow mustard

⅛ teaspoon kosher salt

¼ teaspoon granulated monk fruit sweetener

Caramelized Onions

1 tablespoon salted butter

1 large yellow onion, diced

Kosher salt

Freshly ground black pepper

1 teaspoon balsamic vinegar

Burgers

1½ pounds 85% lean ground beef

Kosher salt

1 tablespoon extra-virgin olive oil

4 slices American cheese, preferably Kraft Deli Deluxe

For Serving

4 cups mixed greens or lettuce

1 cup halved cherry tomatoes

Dill pickles

Yellow hot chili peppers

1. Make the special sauce: In a small bowl, combine the mayo, ketchup, pickle brine, relish, mustard, salt, and monk fruit sweetener. Mix well until smooth and adjust the seasoning to taste.

2. Prepare the caramelized onions: In a large skillet, melt the butter over medium heat. Add the onion and season with salt and pepper. Cook the onions, stirring occasionally, until tender and translucent, about 10 minutes. Reduce the heat to low, add the balsamic vinegar, and continue cooking, stirring frequently, until the onions are caramelized and golden brown, about 15 minutes. Set aside.

(recipe continues)

Makes 4 servings * **Total time:** about 30 minutes
Per serving * **Calories:** 480 * **Protein:** 37g * **Carbohydrates:** 11g * **Fat:** 31g

3. Make the burgers: In a large bowl, season the ground beef generously with salt. Divide the ground beef into 4 equal portions. Roll into balls and set aside.

4. Place a large skillet over medium heat. Add the oil and heat until shimmering. Place one ball of ground beef into the skillet. Then, using a metal spatula (or a meat press), press down firmly on the beef to create a thin, flat patty. Hold the spatula in place for 10 seconds. Then allow the beef to sit undisturbed for 1 to 2 minutes, until a crust forms.

5. Flip the burger, top with a slice of cheese, and add a generous dollop of caramelized onions. Cook until the cheese is melted and the burger is fully cooked, about 2 more minutes. Remove the burger from the pan. Repeat to make 4 burgers.

6. To serve, add 1 cup of salad greens to each of 4 bowls. Place a burger patty on top of the greens and add the tomatoes, pickles, and peppers. Drizzle the special sauce over top.

tip: You can make these bowls with a variety of toppings: try all kinds of pickles, use different flavors of sauce, or swap the onions for caramelized garlic and shallots. For meal prep, make the sauce ahead of time and have it ready in the fridge whenever you want to make a bowl—you'll have dinner ready in 30 minutes!

serving suggestion ✱
To me, meatloaf has to be
served on a bed of something
rich and creamy, like my Garlic
Cauliflower Mash (page 232)
or simple stewed white beans.

In the TV shows I watched growing up, meatloaf always got so much hate. Well, I started making it myself, and now it's become one of my favorite comfort dishes, especially when the weather starts to get cold. Even if you're convinced you don't like meatloaf, give mine a try, then report back.

The balsamic caramelized onions keep this moist and pack it full of flavor.

classic meatloaf

Caramelized Onions

2 tablespoons butter

1 large yellow onion, finely chopped

½ teaspoon kosher salt

1 tablespoon balsamic vinegar

Meatloaf

2 pounds 85% lean ground beef, preferably chuck

3 tablespoons Worcestershire sauce

⅓ cup beef broth

½ cup Italian-style breadcrumbs

2 large eggs

¼ cup chopped fresh parsley

2 teaspoons kosher salt

2 teaspoons mushroom-based umami seasoning blend

½ teaspoon freshly ground black pepper

½ teaspoon garlic powder

½ teaspoon onion powder

Glaze

¼ cup ketchup

2 tablespoons Swerve brown sugar erythritol

1 tablespoon balsamic vinegar

1. **Make the caramelized onions:** Set a medium skillet over medium heat and add the butter. Once the butter melts, add the onion and salt and cook, stirring occasionally, until the onions are soft and caramelized, 10 to 15 minutes.

2. Reduce the heat slightly and stir in the balsamic vinegar. Cook for about 3 more minutes, stirring occasionally, until the balsamic reduces. Remove the pan from the heat and let cool slightly.

3. **Make the meatloaf:** Preheat the oven to 375°F. Line a sheet pan with parchment paper.

4. In a large bowl, combine the ground beef, caramelized onions, Worcestershire sauce, beef broth, breadcrumbs, eggs, parsley, salt, umami seasoning, black pepper, garlic powder, and onion powder. Mix until just combined. Avoid overmixing—you don't want your meatloaf to be tough.

5. Transfer the meatloaf mixture to the prepared sheet pan and shape it into a large loaf. Transfer to the oven and bake for 45 minutes.

6. **Meanwhile, make the glaze:** In a small bowl, stir together the ketchup, Swerve, and balsamic vinegar.

7. After 45 minutes, spread the glaze over the meatloaf. Return the meatloaf to the oven to continue baking until the meat reaches an internal temperature of 160°F, about 20 more minutes.

8. Remove the meatloaf from the oven and let it rest for 10 minutes before slicing and serving.

Makes 8 servings * **Total time:** about 1 hour 45 minutes
Per serving * **Calories:** 320 * **Protein:** 26g * **Carbohydrates:** 20g * **Fat:** 16g

If it isn't apparent already, I love to add a little spice where I can (or sometimes a lot of it). These meatballs are made with ground beef, hot Italian sausage, and Calabrian chiles and are simmered in a spicy arrabbiata tomato sauce. If spice isn't your thing, everything can easily be adjusted: you can use "mild" or "sweet" sausage, leave out the chilis, and swap the arrabbiata sauce for marinara. You can really use any store-bought or homemade arrabbiata or marinara sauce—Rao's is just my personal favorite.

spicy jumbo italian meatballs

1 pound 85% lean ground beef

1 pound bulk hot Italian sausage (see Note)

1 tablespoon chopped Calabrian chiles in oil

¼ cup chopped fresh parsley, plus more for garnish

¼ cup grated Parmesan cheese, plus more for garnish

1 teaspoon kosher salt

½ teaspoon freshly ground black pepper

¾ cup Italian-style breadcrumbs

2 large eggs

2 (24-ounce) jars Rao's arrabbiata sauce, or your marinara sauce of choice

1. Preheat the oven to 425°F. Line a sheet pan with parchment paper.

2. Make the meatballs: In a large bowl, combine the ground beef, Italian sausage, Calabrian chiles, parsley, Parmesan, salt, black pepper, breadcrumbs, and eggs. Mix until just combined.

3. Using clean, washed hands, divide the mixture into 8 equal portions (about 4 ounces each) and roll into meatballs.

4. Place the meatballs on the prepared sheet pan. Transfer to the oven and bake until the tops of the meatballs have slightly browned and some of the fat has cooked out of the meat, about 15 minutes. Remove from the oven and set aside.

5. In a large pot, bring the arrabbiata sauce to a simmer over low heat. Carefully add the baked meatballs to the pot of sauce, browned-side up. Cover and simmer over low heat until the meatballs are cooked through, about 30 minutes.

6. Serve the meatballs in the sauce, garnished with more Parmesan cheese and parsley.

note: If you can only find sausage links (as opposed to bulk sausage), simply cut them open, remove the meat, and discard the casings.

serving suggestion ✻
Serve with a side salad for a delicious weekend dinner.

Makes 8 servings (8 large meatballs) ✻ **Total time:** about 1 hour 20 minutes
Per serving ✻ **Calories:** 460 ✻ **Protein:** 28g ✻ **Carbohydrates:** 24g ✻ **Fat:** 26g

I guess I got my inspiration for cooking my cravings from my mom. I remember her taking me and my little brother to Taco Bell in our minivan when we were little. We'd find a shady spot under a tree and eat our Taco Bell in the car. It was one of my brother's favorite meals (actually one of the only things he'd eat, since he was such a picky eater). To keep him happy, my mom started recreating Taco Bell meals at home, and it quickly became a favorite dinner for all of us.

This recipe was inspired by the Taco Bell Enchirito—a delicious mash-up between a burrito and an enchilada that is sadly no longer on the menu. It was my mom's favorite thing to order, and here I am, over fifteen years later, including my mom's Enchirito recipe in my cookbook. It's still a favorite to this day, and I've never served it to anyone who wasn't instantly hooked.

taco bell–inspired smothered "burritos"

1½ pounds 85% lean ground beef

1 (1-ounce) packet McCormick taco seasoning, or your favorite taco seasoning blend

1 (16-ounce) can refried beans

6 (10-inch) low-carb flour tortillas

2 cups shredded Mexican cheese blend

2 (15-ounce) cans red enchilada sauce

For Serving

Shredded iceberg lettuce

Pickled jalapeños

Pico de gallo

Whole-milk Greek yogurt or sour cream

1. Preheat the oven to 375°F.

2. Set a large skillet over medium-high heat. Add the ground beef and cook until browned, about 10 minutes, using a spatula to break up large chunks. Drain off any excess fat.

3. Add the taco seasoning (and any water called for in the packet instructions) and stir to incorporate. Cook according to the seasoning packet instructions, usually about 5 minutes.

4. Transfer the refried beans to a medium microwave-safe dish. Microwave the beans in 30-second intervals, stirring after each interval, until heated through.

5. Wrap the tortillas in damp paper towels. Microwave for 30 seconds to 1 minute to steam them—this will make them more pliable and easier to roll.

(recipe continues)

Makes 6 servings * Total time: about 50 minutes
Per serving * Calories: 540 * Protein: 40g * Carbohydrates: 42g * Fat: 26g

6. Lay the tortillas on a flat work surface. Spread a thin layer of refried beans in the center of each tortilla. Sprinkle 1 cup of shredded cheese over the beans (about 2 tablespoons on each tortilla). Spoon the seasoned ground beef mixture on top of the cheese and beans. Tightly roll the tortillas into burritos and line them up seam-sides down in a 9 by 13-inch baking dish.

7. Pour the red enchilada sauce evenly over the rolled tortillas and sprinkle them with the remaining 1 cup of shredded cheese.

8. Cover the baking dish with aluminum foil and bake in the oven for 20 minutes. Remove the foil and continue baking until the cheese is melted and bubbly, an additional 10 minutes.

9. Let the burritos cool for a few minutes before serving. Serve topped with shredded lettuce, pickeled jalapeños, pico de gallo, and a dollop of Greek yogurt.

These lettuce wraps are insanely delicious, low-carb, and a refreshing summertime dinner idea! I always love ground beef, and the peanut sauce takes this dish to the next level. It's an incredible recipe that uses peanut butter powder, which keeps the fat and calories a bit lower without compromising on flavor.

The water chestnuts give you such a nice crunch alongside the crispy lettuce. You can use ground chicken, pork, or turkey if you prefer. You can also meal-prep the peanut sauce and meat, and wrap it in fresh lettuce throughout the week as you eat.

ground beef lettuce wraps

Peanut Sauce

½ cup powdered peanut butter

1 tablespoon coconut aminos

1 tablespoon seasoned rice vinegar

1 teaspoon toasted sesame oil

½ teaspoon garlic powder

½ teaspoon ground ginger

2 teaspoons sriracha

2 teaspoons hot honey

Beef Filling

1½ pounds 85% lean ground beef

3 garlic cloves, minced

1 teaspoon minced fresh ginger

3 tablespoons coconut aminos

1 tablespoon oyster sauce

1 tablespoon seasoned rice vinegar

1 (8-ounce) can water chestnuts, drained and finely chopped

3 green onions, sliced, whites and greens separated

For Serving

1 head butter or romaine lettuce, leaves separated

Sesame seeds, for garnish (optional)

Chopped fresh cilantro, for garnish (optional)

1. **Make the peanut sauce:** In a small bowl, combine the peanut butter powder and ¼ cup of water. Stir until the mixture is smooth and creamy. Add the coconut aminos, rice vinegar, sesame oil, garlic powder, ginger, siracha, and hot honey. Stir until well combined and set aside.

(recipe continues)

Makes 4 servings * **Total time:** about 30 minutes
Per serving * **Calories:** 450 * **Protein:** 40g * **Carbohydrates:** 26g * **Fat:** 20g

serving suggestion *
Serve with Not-Smashed
Cucumber Salad (page 231).

2. Make the beef filling: Set a large skillet over medium-high heat. When the skillet is hot, add the ground beef and cook until browned and cooked through, 8 to 10 minutes, using a spatula to break up any large pieces. Drain off any excess fat. Add the garlic and ginger and cook until just fragrant, another 1 minute.

3. In a small bowl, whisk together the coconut aminos, rice vinegar, and oyster sauce. Pour the sauce mixture into the skillet with the beef mixture. Stir in the water chestnuts and the whites of the green onions. Cook for an additional 4 to 5 minutes to allow the flavors to meld together.

4. Assemble the wraps: Arrange the lettuce leaves on a serving platter. Spoon the beef filling into the center of each lettuce leaf. Garnish with the remaining green onions. If desired, garnish with sesame seeds and fresh cilantro. Serve alongside the peanut sauce for dipping.

My boyfriend and I are huge Korean BBQ fans. It's one of our favorite date-night dinners, and with plenty of protein and a few varieties of kimchi and other vegetable banchan side dishes, it's a perfectly balanced meal in my book. One of one of my favorite Korean BBQ dishes is kalbi (or galbi), which are grilled ribs.

You'll need long, flanken-cut ribs, usually cut no more than ½ inch thick, with cross-sections of bone.

This is a non-traditional, shortcut version of kalbi. Traditional marinades are often made with Asian pear, honey, and soy sauce. I like to use coconut aminos because they provide a natural sweetness. Along with fresh ginger and garlic, they make an easy and incredibly flavorful marinade. The longer you can let the ribs marinate, the better—you'll be chewing every last bite off the bone.

Some people like to cook short ribs to medium-rare, but I find the meat gets more tender if they cook longer, plus, you can create a nice char.

shortcut korean-style short ribs

1 cup coconut aminos

1 teaspoon toasted sesame oil

3 garlic cloves, minced

2 teaspoons minced fresh ginger

2 pounds flanken-style short ribs

Kosher salt

Freshly ground black pepper

Neutral oil, for grill

For Serving

2 green onions, thinly sliced

serving suggestion *
These short ribs are typically served with kimchi, other cold vegetables, salad, or white rice, but at home, we usually eat them with scallion pancakes.

1. **Make the marinade:** In a large resealable ziplock bag or shallow dish, combine the coconut aminos, sesame oil, garlic, and ginger.

2. Add the short ribs to the marinade, ensuring they are well coated. Seal the bag (or cover the dish) and place in the fridge to marinate for at least 4 hours, or, for best results, overnight.

3. Preheat the grill to medium heat and oil the grates.

4. Remove the short ribs from the marinade and let any excess marinade drip off. Season both sides of the ribs with salt and pepper.

5. Place the short ribs on the grill. Close the grill and cook for 5 minutes. Rotate the ribs (this way, you'll get crosshatched grill marks), then close the grill and cook for 5 more minutes. Flip the ribs and repeat the process on the other side, for a total grill time of 20 minutes. Turn the ribs occasionally to ensure even cooking and prevent burning.

6. Let the short ribs rest for a few minutes, then garnish with green onions and serve.

Makes 6 servings * **Total time:** about 30 minutes, plus 4 hours marinating time
Per serving * **Calories:** 380 * **Protein:** 16g * **Carbohydrates:** 7g * **Fat:** 31g

When I see a cut of meat at the grocery store that I haven't cooked before, chances are I'm going to impulse-buy it and figure out the rest later. So when I spotted a giant rack of dino ribs at Costco, I couldn't resist. A beef lover's dream! Plus, they're budget-friendly; I was able to pick up a hefty rack for around $25. While they do come with a fair amount of bone, the meat is incredibly flavorful.

Even though I'd never made them before, I figured you could never go wrong cooking ribs low and slow. They came out delicious, so I decided to keep the recipe simple. These ribs are surprisingly easy to make—the oven does most of the work, and you need just a few ingredients. You might feel like a caveman at first eating them straight off the bone, but trust me, you'll find yourself reaching for more.

slow-roasted dino ribs

1 (4-pound) rack beef "dino" ribs

1 tablespoon extra-virgin olive oil

Black & Tan Steak Seasoning, or other steak seasoning of your choice

1. Preheat the oven to 300°F.

2. Rinse the ribs and pat them dry with paper towels. Using a sharp knife, score the back of the ribs to cut through and remove the membrane.

3. Coat the ribs with olive oil on both sides and season them generously with steak seasoning.

4. Place the ribs in a large roasting pan or baking dish, bone-side up. Cover the pan tightly with aluminum foil.

5. Transfer to the oven and bake until the ribs are tender and the meat is pulling away from the bones, about 4 hours.

6. After 4 hours, remove the aluminum foil, flip the ribs, and set the oven to broil. Broil the ribs until they are crispy and browned around the edges, 3 to 5 minutes.

7. Remove from the oven and let the ribs rest for 10 minutes before slicing and serving.

serving suggestion * These ribs pair well with mashed potatoes, Balsamic Brussels Sprouts (page 239), or roasted red cabbage.

Makes 8 servings * **Total time:** about 4 hours 20 minutes
Per serving * **Calories:** 470 * **Protein:** 30g * **Carbohydrates:** 0g * **Fat:** 38g

This is an easy and healthy take on Chinese takeout fried rice. Using cauliflower instead of the usual white rice makes this a low-carb dish, but if you prefer, the recipe will also work with cold, leftover rice. I use frozen peas and carrots because they cook quickly, but you can really add in any veggies you have on hand, like broccoli or mushrooms.

I wrote this recipe to be made in a large skillet or wok, but if you have one, I've started to cook this at home on a flat-top griddle, hibachi-style. The larger surface area will give you a better sear on the ingredients. I make a yogurt-based, tomatoey take on yum yum sauce, and I think it's so delicious drizzled on top of the rice.

cauliflower fried rice
with yum yum sauce

Yum Yum Sauce

¼ cup whole-milk Greek yogurt

¼ cup light mayonnaise

1 tablespoon tomato paste

1 tablespoon seasoned rice vinegar

½ teaspoon garlic powder

½ teaspoon onion powder

¼ teaspoon smoked paprika

½ tablespoon granulated monk fruit sweetener

Fried Rice

1 pound 85% lean ground beef

4 garlic cloves, minced

1 teaspoon minced fresh ginger

4 green onions, chopped, whites and greens separated

4 cups cauliflower rice, thawed if frozen

½ cup frozen peas and carrots blend

1 tablespoon salted butter

2 large eggs

¼ cup coconut aminos

2 teaspoons toasted sesame oil

1 teaspoon kosher salt

½ teaspoon freshly ground black pepper

1. Make the yum yum sauce: In a small bowl, combine the yogurt, mayo, tomato paste, rice vinegar, garlic powder, onion powder, smoked paprika, monk fruit sweetener, and ¼ cup of water. Mix until completely smooth and refrigerate until ready to serve.

2. Make the fried rice: Set a heavy 12-inch skillet over medium-high heat. Add the ground beef and cook until browned, 8 to 10 minutes, using a heavy spatula to break apart any large pieces.

(recipe continues)

Makes 4 servings * Total time: about 45 minutes
Per serving * Calories: 410 * Protein: 29g * Carbohydrates: 20g * Fat: 23g

serving suggestion ✴ This could easily be a main course, especially if you add more vegetables, but you can also serve it with another protein, like Air-Fryer Chicken Dumpling Meatballs (page 90).

3. Add in the garlic, ginger, and the whites of the green onions. Stir for about 1 minute, or until fragrant.

4. Add the cauliflower rice and the peas and carrots to the skillet and mix until well incorporated. Use the spatula to push away the vegetables to make a space in the center of the skillet, so you can cook the eggs. Add the butter to the empty spot in the center of the skillet; once it has melted, crack both eggs into it. Let the eggs cook until the whites are just set; then scramble the eggs in the center of the skillet before mixing them into the rice.

5. Add the coconut aminos, sesame oil, salt, pepper, and remaining green onions to the skillet and cook everything together, stirring frequently, for another 4 to 5 minutes, or until everything is incorporated and the liquid has cooked off.

6. Divide the beef fried rice among bowls and serve hot, drizzled with yum yum sauce (or with sauce on the side).

Whenever I'm craving lasagna, this is the recipe I make. I love that it's made low-carb—since zucchini is used in place of lasagna noodles—but it's still so full of flavor. Since zucchini releases liquid (rather than absorbing it like a lasagna noodle would), you'll want to sprinkle it with a little salt before cooking to draw out some moisture ahead of time. Doing this first will also give it a better chance of holding up during cooking.

Most lasagnas use ricotta, but here, I use pesto blended with cottage cheese. It adds so much flavor and pairs nicely with the other ingredients. I don't think you'll miss the ricotta, but if you have some on hand, you're welcome to use it instead of cottage cheese. This recipe makes great leftovers to reheat and eat during the week.

zucchini lasagna

4 large zucchinis, ends trimmed

Kosher salt

1½ teaspoons extra-virgin olive oil

1 large yellow onion, finely chopped

4 garlic cloves, minced

2 pounds 85% lean ground beef

1 (32-ounce) jar Rao's marinara sauce, or your marinara sauce of choice

Kosher salt

¼ teaspoon freshly ground black pepper

2 cup low-fat cottage cheese

¼ cup store-bought pesto

¼ cup grated Parmesan cheese

1 large egg

½ cup shredded mozzarella cheese

1. **Prep the zucchini:** Line a large sheet pan with paper towels. Using a mandolin, carefully slice the zucchini lengthwise into thin slices, resembling lasagna noodles. Set the slices on the prepared sheet pan. Lightly salt them, let them sit 15 minutes, and then blot with paper towels to remove moisture.

2. **Make the meat sauce:** Set a large skillet over medium heat and add the olive oil. Once the oil is hot, add the onion and cook, stirring occasionally, until softened, 3 to 4 minutes. Add the garlic and cook for another 30 seconds, until fragrant. Add the beef and stir, using a heavy spatula to break up any large pieces. Cook until browned, 7 to 10 minutes. Drain any excess fat.

3. Stir in the marinara sauce, ½ teaspoon salt, and black pepper. Let the mixture simmer until everything is heated through, 7 to 10 minutes. Remove from the heat and set aside.

4. **Make the cheese mixture:** In a small blender or food processor, combine the cottage cheese, pesto, Parmesan, and egg. Blend until smooth and well combined. Set aside.

5. Preheat the oven to 375°F. Lightly grease a 9 by 13-inch baking dish.

(recipe continues)

Makes 8 servings * Total time: about 2 hours
Per serving * Calories: 440 * Protein: 34g * Carbohydrates: 14g * Fat: 17g

serving suggestion ✳ I like to pair this with a simple salad.

6. Assemble the lasagna: Spread a thin layer of meat sauce over the bottom of the baking dish. Place the zucchini slices across the bottom of the dish, slightly overlapping the slices to form a solid layer. Spread more meat sauce over the zucchini. Pour the cheese mixture over the meat sauce and spread it in an even layer. Add another layer of zucchini slices on top of the cheese mixture, then a meat layer, and so on. Repeat this layering—zucchini, then meat sauce, then cheese mixture—until all ingredients are used, finishing with a layer of zucchini slices on top.

7. Sprinkle the mozzarella evenly over the lasagna.

8. Cover the lasagna with aluminum foil. Transfer to the oven and bake for 45 minutes. Remove the foil, set the oven to broil, and broil just until the top is golden brown, about 1 minute.

9. Let the lasagna cool for 10 minutes before slicing and serving.

serving suggestion
✱ Serve with corn salsa to add freshness to the rich and spicy barbacoa. If you prefer a side of roasted or grilled corn on the cob, top with a little Greek yogurt and Cotija cheese for an elote-style take.

I grew up eating Mexican food, and barbacoa tacos were one of my mom's favorite dishes. This recipe uses barbacoa in quesadillas, for more protein and, let's face it, cheese! Some food historians believe that barbacoa cooking is how BBQ originated. In Mexico, barbacoa refers to a method of slow-cooking in a fire pit—a hole in the ground lined with hot stones and covered with leaves.

With that in mind, I wanted to cook the meat for this recipe in a slow cooker, which allows the flavors from the adobo sauce and spices to mingle with the beef. Slow-cooking chuck roast is key so it gets tender—that way, you can easily shred the meat with forks. You could also make this recipe with pork shoulder, which is often slightly cheaper.

slow-cooker barbacoa quesadillas

Slow-Cooker Barbacoa

3 pounds beef chuck roast, cut into 4 large chunks

1 tablespoon neutral oil

1 (14.5-ounce) can diced fire-roasted tomatoes

2 whole chipotle peppers in adobo sauce

1 cup beef broth

2 tablespoons fresh lime juice

2 tablespoons honey

4 garlic cloves, minced

2 teaspoons ground cumin

2 teaspoons kosher salt

Quesadillas

12 (10-inch) low-carb flour tortillas

4 cups shredded quesadilla cheese

For Serving

Pickled red onions

Chopped fresh cilantro

1. Set a large skillet over medium-high heat and add the neutral oil. Add the cut-up chuck roast and sear on all sides until well browned, about 15 minutes. Set aside.

2. Make the barbacoa marinade: In a blender or food processor, combine the diced tomatoes, chipotle peppers, beef broth, lime juice, honey, garlic, cumin, and salt. Blend until smooth.

3. Transfer the seared beef and the marinade to a slow cooker. Cook on high for 4 hours (or low for 8 hours), or until the beef is tender and easily shredded with a fork.

4. Remove the beef from the slow cooker and shred it using two forks. Return the shredded beef to the slow cooker and stir it back into the broth. Taste, and add more salt if desired.

5. Make the quesadillas: Set a large skillet or two (to make two at a time) over medium heat. Place a tortilla in the skillet and spread roughly ⅓ cup of shredded barbacoa beef over half of it. Top with shredded cheese and fold the tortilla closed. Cook until the cheese is melted and the tortilla is golden brown and crispy on both sides, 2 to 3 minutes per side, and remove from the pan. Repeat to make 12 quesadillas.

6. To serve, slice quesadillas into wedges and garnish with pickled red onions and cilantro.

Makes 12 quesadillas * Total time: about 5 hours
Per quesadilla * Calories: 520 * Protein: 42g * Carbohydrates: 23g * Fat: 32g

seafood

I've heard people say salmon is too "fishy," but I'm betting most of them just haven't had salmon that's cooked well. I look for thicker cuts, which can be cooked medium-rare if you prefer. I once turned to my copy of *The Flavor Bible* (Yes, it's a real book—and a classic at that!) to look for flavors that pair well with salmon, and I found that Dijon mustard was the ideal match. What's more, mustard was the perfect way to make seasonings stick to the fish. The Old Bay and smoked paprika in this recipe give it a rich, smoky flavor.

With only a handful of ingredients, this dish is super quick to get to the table. It's my favorite way to eat salmon—the recipe quickly went viral and is one of my most-cooked recipes to this day. If you buy Old Bay just for this recipe, know that it goes well on all kinds of fish and seafood and can be used to season vegetables.

smoky air-fryer old bay–mustard salmon

4 (6-ounce) salmon fillets, skin-on

2 tablespoons Dijon mustard

2 teaspoons Old Bay seasoning

2 teaspoons smoked paprika

2 tablespoons salted butter, melted

2 garlic cloves, minced

Kosher salt

Freshly ground black pepper

Juice of ½ lemon, for serving

1. Preheat the air fryer to 400°F for about 5 minutes.

2. Lightly brush each salmon fillet with Dijon mustard. Sprinkle both sides evenly with Old Bay and smoked paprika.

3. Place the salmon fillets in a single layer in the air-fryer basket, cooking in batches if needed. Cook until the salmon has a nice crust on top and flakes easily with a fork, about 8 minutes.

4. Meanwhile, make the garlic butter: In a small saucepan, melt the butter over medium heat. Add the garlic and cook for about 1 minute, stirring occasionally, until fragrant. Season with salt and pepper.

5. To serve, place the salmon on serving plates and drizzle evenly with the garlic butter. Serve with the lemon.

tip: If you're a fan of salmon skin, cooking the salmon in the air fryer makes the skin really crispy. I am personally not a massive fan of the skin, but you know who is? My dogs. I give them the skin for a nice treat, and it's also great for their fur—a win-win. To remove the skin from the cooked fish (be sure to leave it on during cooking), simply lift the edge of the skin, slide a fork along the inside, and peel it off.

serving suggestion ★
Salmon is versatile, so this can be made into a meal with all kinds of sides, including salad or roasted vegetables like okra, sweet potatoes, or zucchini.

Makes 4 servings ★ **Total time:** about 25 minutes
Per serving ★ **Calories:** 340 ★ **Protein:** 39g ★ **Carbohydrates:** 2g ★ **Fat:** 18g

I get why so many people deep-fry shrimp—it's an attempt to make up for blandness. But I think there are ways to let the hidden flavors of the shrimp shine. The chile-lime seasoning and lime juice enhances their subtle sweetness and briny, ocean-like taste. The result is a perfectly balanced bite that's anything but bland. If you can find Argentinian red shrimp, grab them—they have an almost lobster-like flavor. There are a few good chile-lime seasonings on the market. The classic is Tajín, but I also love the ones available from Trader Joe's or Simply Organic.

grilled chile-lime shrimp skewers
with creamy chipotle sauce

2 tablespoons extra-virgin olive oil

4 garlic cloves, minced

2 tablespoons chopped fresh cilantro

1 tablespoon chile-lime seasoning

2 pounds large shrimp, peeled and deveined

Neutral oil, for grill

Chipotle Yogurt Sauce, for serving (page 40)

1. In a large bowl, combine the olive oil, garlic, cilantro, and chile-lime seasoning. Add the shrimp to the bowl and toss to coat evenly. Marinate for up to 4 hours.

2. If using wooden skewers, soak them in water for at least 30 minutes before grilling to prevent burning.

3. Preheat the grill to high heat and oil the grates.

4. In the meantime, prepare the Chipotle Yogurt Sauce.

5. Thread the marinated shrimp onto the skewers, leaving a little space between each to allow for even cooking. Place the shrimp skewers on the grill and cook until the shrimp are opaque and slightly charred, 1 to 2 minutes per side max. The shrimp cook quickly, so don't leave them too long because they'll get rubbery and lose flavor if they're overcooked. Once they're pink and feel barely firm, they're done!

6. Serve the grilled shrimp hot with the Chipotle Yogurt Sauce on the side for dipping.

serving suggestion ★ These skewers can also be turned into tacos for an easy weekday meal. Garnish with sliced avocado and serve with yellow rice, black beans, and salad.

Makes 4 servings ★ **Total time:** about 30 minutes
Per serving ★ **Calories:** 280 ★ **Protein:** 40g ★ **Carbohydrates:** 4g ★ **Fat:** 10g

The key to this quick, easy, undeniably delicious dish lies in the deceptively simple teriyaki-inspired marinade. The honey and coconut aminos help the salmon caramelize on the outside while staying tender and juicy on the inside. I recommend marinating the salmon for a couple hours if you can, but if you're short on time, 30 minutes will suffice.

air-fryer teriyaki salmon bites

¼ cup coconut aminos

1 tablespoon honey

1 teaspoon toasted sesame oil

½ teaspoon garlic salt

1½ pounds salmon fillets, skinned, cut into bite-size pieces

For Serving

Sliced green onions

Sesame seeds

1. **Make the marinade:** In a medium bowl, combine the coconut aminos, honey, sesame oil, and garlic salt. Mix well.

2. Place the salmon pieces in a shallow dish or a resealable ziplock bag. Pour the marinade over the salmon, ensuring all pieces are well coated. Marinate in the fridge for at least 30 minutes, but preferably 2 to 4 hours.

3. Preheat the air fryer to 400°F for about 5 minutes.

4. Remove the salmon from the marinade and allow any excess marinade to drip off. Place the salmon pieces in the air-fryer basket in a single layer. Depending on the size of your air fryer, you may need to cook in batches.

5. Air-fry the salmon until it is cooked through and has a nice, crispy exterior, 6 to 8 minutes. To ensure even cooking, give the basket a shake halfway through cooking.

6. Transfer the salmon to a serving dish. Garnish with sesame seeds and green onions and serve hot.

serving suggestion ★ I love to pair these salmon bites with rice or Garlic-Herb Cauliflower Rice (page 236) and some stir-fried vegetables like broccoli, onions, and edamame. You could also do roast cabbage or steamed bok choy—enjoy on the side or serve everything together in a bowl.

Makes 6 servings ★ **Total time:** about 15 minutes, plus 30 minutes marinating time

Per serving ★ **Calories:** 280 ★ **Protein:** 40g ★ **Carbohydrates:** 8g ★ **Fat:** 10g

My mom and I used go to Outback Steakhouse, and my go-to order was a similar version of this dish. The difference in cost between the restaurant dish and my homemade ahi tuna is substantial, but truth be told, when I see it on a restaurant menu, I still sometimes let myself indulge. I just can't get enough!

This was one of the first recipes I ever posted on social media, and the response gave me a big morale boost. I'm so thankful for those memories of my early days on social media and even more grateful to be able to share this recipe with you!

sesame-crusted tuna
with soy-ginger dressing

Soy-Ginger Dressing

¼ cup soy sauce

1 tablespoon seasoned rice vinegar

1 teaspoon toasted sesame oil

1 teaspoon grated fresh ginger

2 garlic cloves, minced

1 teaspoon honey

Tuna

¼ cup black sesame seeds

¼ cup white sesame seeds

4 (4-ounce) ahi tuna steaks

Kosher salt

Freshly ground black pepper

2 tablespoons extra-virgin olive oil

serving suggestion ✳ To turn this into a complete meal, serve over rice (or cauliflower rice), and top with sliced cucumber, diced or pickled red onion, sliced avocado, carrot ribbons, and more sesame seeds and green onions.

1. Make the soy-ginger dressing: In a small bowl, combine the soy sauce, rice vinegar, sesame oil, ginger, garlic, and honey. Mix well until the honey is completely dissolved.

2. Prepare the tuna: On a large plate, stir together the black and white sesame seeds. Pat the ahi tuna steaks dry with paper towels. Season them well with salt and pepper. Press each tuna steak into the sesame seed mixture on both sides, until evenly coated with sesame seeds.

3. Set a nonstick skillet over high heat. Once the skillet is very hot, add the oil and swirl to coat the skillet. Add the sesame-crusted tuna steaks and cook until the seeds begin to toast and a sear forms, 1 to 2 minutes. Flip and repeat on the other side. Work quickly to ensure you get a crispy outside while keeping the inside raw.

4. Let the tuna steaks rest for a few minutes before thinly slicing them against the grain. Drizzle the soy-ginger dressing over the sliced tuna (or serve it on the side for dipping). Enjoy immediately.

tip: I keep frozen tuna steaks on hand so I can make this whenever a craving hits. But I don't like to thaw fish in the vacuum-sealed plastic packaging that frozen fish is usually sold in. Instead, I unwrap the fish and put it on a covered plate, then leave that plate in the fridge to thaw overnight.

Makes 4 servings ✳ Total time: about 15 minutes
Per serving ✳ Calories: 310 ✳ Protein: 32g ✳ Carbohydrates: 8g ✳ Fat: 17g

serving suggestion
✱ Serve this dish with sautéed asparagus and broccoli or serve over cauliflower mash.

To be honest, I only enjoy spinach when it's sautéed or cooked in some kind of cream sauce. That might defeat the purpose of eating spinach in the first place, but either way, it's still delicious. The sauce for this smoky roasted salmon is my take on creamed spinach, adding Parmesan and spicy Calabrian chiles to turn the flavor up. If you don't have Calabrian chiles, just use a teaspoon or two of crushed red pepper flakes to add some heat. This sauce would work great with chicken, too. If you want to switch it up, switch out the spinach for kale and top with bacon.

salmon
with spicy creamed spinach sauce

Salmon

2 teaspoons smoked paprika

1 teaspoon Swerve brown sugar erythritol

1 teaspoon dried parsley

Kosher salt

Freshly ground black pepper

4 (6-ounce) salmon fillets, skin removed

1 tablespoon extra-virgin olive oil

Spicy Creamed Spinach Sauce

2 tablespoons salted butter

3 garlic cloves, minced

½ teaspoon red pepper flakes

¾ cup heavy cream

¾ cup grated Parmesan cheese

¼ cup chicken broth

1 tablespoon chopped Calabrian chiles in oil

2 cups finely chopped spinach

Kosher salt

Freshly ground black pepper

1. Preheat the oven to 400°F. Line a sheet pan with parchment paper.

2. **Make the spice mixture:** In a small bowl, combine the smoked paprika, Swerve, parsley, 2 teaspoons salt, and ½ teaspoon pepper.

3. **Cook the salmon:** Place the salmon fillets on the prepared sheet pan. Coat the fillets with the oil and season with the spice mixture. Gently press the seasonings into the fillets to adhere. Transfer to the oven and bake until the salmon flakes apart easily, with a slightly shiny pink center, about 12 minutes.

4. **Meanwhile, make the spicy creamed spinach sauce:** In a large skillet, melt the butter over medium heat. Add the garlic and red pepper flakes and sauté for 1 to 2 minutes, until just fragrant. Pour in the heavy cream and bring to a simmer. Let the heavy cream simmer for 3 to 4 minutes, until slightly thickened.

5. Add the Parmesan and chicken broth, and stir until the Parmesan is melted and the sauce is smooth, 1 to 2 minutes. Stir in the Calabrian chilis and spinach and cook until the spinach is wilted, 4 to 5 minutes. The sauce should be thick enough so that it can easily coat the back of a spoon. Season with salt and pepper to taste.

6. To serve, transfer the salmon to plates. Spoon the spicy creamed spinach sauce over the top of each fillet and enjoy immediately.

Makes 4 servings ∗ **Total time:** about 30 minutes
Per serving ∗ **Calories:** 550 ∗ **Protein:** 47g ∗ **Carbohydrates:** 7g ∗ **Fat:** 39g

I used to be intimidated by cooking curry because the flavors are so bold and complex, but that's exactly what makes them irresistible. The balance of heat, creaminess, and spice creates a rich and comforting dish that's hard to beat. The first time I tried curry was on vacation at a resort in the Florida Keys with my boyfriend. I had a Caribbean-inspired curry made with yellowfin tuna and curry powder. Since then, I've fallen in love with all kinds of curries, including Thai curries. Instead of curry powders, they tend to use pounded pastes full of herbs and chiles, which I've come to prefer for their intense flavor.

This recipe uses Thai red curry paste with salmon—I think it enhances the natural sweetness of the fish and pairs beautifully with the warm, vibrant flavors of coconut, ginger, and garlic. This preparation would work great with any meaty fish, including mahi-mahi, halibut, tilapia, or cod. This is a luxurious but also comforting and quick dinner—in just 30 minutes, you'll have a flavorful, satisfying meal right in front of you!

coconut curry salmon

4 (6-ounce) salmon fillets, skin removed

Kosher salt

Freshly ground black pepper

1 tablespoon extra-virgin olive oil

2 garlic cloves, minced

1 teaspoon minced fresh ginger

2 tablespoons Thai red curry paste

1 (14-ounce) can full-fat coconut milk

1 teaspoon fish sauce

1 tablespoon hot honey

Juice of 1 lime

1 tablespoon Swerve brown sugar erythritol

For Serving

Chopped fresh cilantro

1. Season the salmon filets with salt and pepper.

2. Sear the salmon: Set a large skillet with a lid over medium-low heat and add the olive oil. Once the olive oil is hot, add the salmon fillets and sear until golden brown on both sides, about 2 minutes per side. You do not want to fully cook the salmon at this point. You just want to develop a crust; the salmon will finish cooking in the sauce. Remove the salmon from the skillet and set aside.

3. Make the curry sauce: To the same skillet, add the garlic and ginger and sauté for about 1 minute or until fragrant. Add the curry paste and cook, stirring constantly, for 1 to 2 minutes, until it turns a shade darker. Pour in the coconut milk and stir to incorporate.

4. Add in the fish sauce, hot honey, lime juice, and Swerve and stir well. Bring the sauce to a gentle simmer and cook for 5 minutes, until slightly thickened.

5. Return the seared salmon fillets to the skillet, nestling them into the curry sauce. Spoon some of the sauce over the salmon to coat it. Cover the skillet with a lid and let the salmon cook in the curry sauce until the sauce can easily coat the back of a spoon

Makes 4 servings * **Total time:** about 35 minutes
Per serving * **Calories:** 490 * **Protein:** 42g * **Carbohydrates:** 14g * **Fat:** 33g

and has reduced by about a quarter, 5 to 10 minutes. Continue simmering until the salmon is cooked through—this timing depends on the thickness of your fillets; check every few minutes. If the fish flakes when pressed with a fork or spatula, it's done.

6. Transfer the salmon to shallow bowls, garnish with cilantro, and serve immediately.

serving suggestion
★ Serve with rice or cauliflower rice and a simple roasted vegetable such as green beans, carrots, or asparagus.

Inspired by shrimp-avocado ceviche, this summery dish of spicy sautéed shrimp and guac on warm tostadas is a quick and easy way to load up with protein. But you can use this recipe in other applications, too: as a salad, over crispy romaine lettuce; as a sandwich, on a crusty baguette; or with a side of roasted vegetables or rice.

shrimp avocado tostadas

4 tostada shells

1½ pounds large shrimp, peeled and deveined

2 tablespoons extra-virgin olive oil

1 teaspoon chili powder

½ teaspoon ground cumin

1 teaspoon dried parsley

1 teaspoon kosher salt

1 tablespoon unsalted butter

For Serving

½ cup guacamole

¼ cup crumbled queso fresco

½ cup thinly sliced pickled red onions

¼ cup chopped fresh cilantro

Lime wedges

1. Preheat the oven to 400°F. Line a sheet pan with parchment paper.

2. Place the tostada shells on the lined sheet pan and bake until warmed and crisp, 3 to 4 minutes.

3. Cook the shrimp: In a large bowl, combine the shrimp, 1 tablespoon olive oil, the chili powder, cumin, parsley, and salt. Mix until the shrimp are evenly coated.

4. Set a large skillet over medium-high heat and add ½ tablespoon butter and 1 tablespoon olive oil. Once the butter is melted, add half of the shrimp in a single layer and cook until they turn pink and opaque, 2 to 3 minutes per side. Remove from the skillet and set aside to cool. Repeat with the remaining shrimp.

5. Assemble the tostadas: Cut the cooked shrimp into small bite-size pieces. Spread about 2 tablespoons of guacamole on each tostada and top with about a quarter of the shrimp pieces. Garnish with queso fresco, pickled red onion, and cilantro and serve with plenty of fresh lime wedges for squeezing on the side.

Makes 4 servings ★ Total time: about 30 minutes
Per serving ★ Calories: 390 ★ Protein: 34g ★ Carbohydrates: 16g ★ Fat: 21g

I love going out to eat, but I always find it hard to order things that I know I can easily cook at home (and for half the price). For that reason, lobster is one of the first things I learned how to make when I was venturing into cooking. I have always had a bit of a bougie flavor palate! If I can learn how to remove the tail from the lobster, you can, too (grab the gloves for this one).

Lobster is a very lean protein, so the garlic butter adds a nice richness to the dish. (I also season the garlic butter with Old Bay and smoked paprika for extra flavor.) This is one of those meals that feels really fancy and high-end, but it's a straightforward process. Once you master it, you can add some surf to any dinner in under 30 minutes.

garlic butter–roasted lobster tails

4 (6-ounce) lobster tails

2 tablespoons salted butter, melted

3 garlic cloves, minced

1 teaspoon dried parsley

½ teaspoon smoked paprika

¼ teaspoon Old Bay seasoning

For Serving
Lemon wedges

1. Preheat the oven to 450°F.

2. **Prep the lobster tails:** Using kitchen shears, and starting at the head end of the lobster, cut lengthwise down the tops of the lobster shells. Stop right before you reach the tail fins. Use your finger to carefully separate the lobster meat from the shell (wear gloves if needed)—but keep the meat attached to the tail fins. When the meat is separated, place it back on the shell, maneuvering the shell so it can lay flat as needed. Place the prepared lobster tails on a sheet pan.

3. **Make the garlic butter:** In a small bowl, combine the butter, garlic, parsley, smoked paprika, and Old Bay. Stir to combine.

4. Brush the lobster tails generously with the garlic butter. Transfer to the oven and bake until the meat is opaque white throughout, 8 to 10 minutes. Set the oven to broil and broil for 1 to 2 minutes. Remove from the oven.

5. Serve the lobster tails hot, with lemon wedges for squeezing.

Makes 4 servings ✳ **Total time:** about 30 minutes
Per serving ✳ **Calories:** 210 ✳ **Protein:** 33g ✳ **Carbohydrates:** 1g ✳ **Fat:** 7g

Umami is a Japanese word that can be translated to "essence of deliciousness." It's used to describe food that has a savory, meaty flavor, but it doesn't always refer to meat. Lots of fish have an umami flavor, as do mushrooms, cheese, and miso paste, which features in this recipe.

Now that we know this dish will be delicious and full of umami, let's get to cooking! In this recipe, you'll coat a fillet of salmon (or other meaty fish, like cod or mahi-mahi) in a glaze of miso, soy sauce, and a little honey. This protects the fish from overcooking and creates a super-flavorful bite. I like to make the salmon in the air fryer since it's so quick, but you could also roast it in the oven at the same temperature, and then broil it for 1 minute to create some nice browning.

air-fryer miso-glazed salmon

¼ cup white miso paste

1 tablespoon soy sauce

1 tablespoon honey

1 tablespoon salted butter, melted

2 tablespoons seasoned rice vinegar

4 (6-ounce) thick-cut, skin-on salmon fillets

For Serving
Lime wedges
Sesame seeds

1. Preheat the air fryer to 375°F for about 5 minutes.

2. Make the glaze: In a small bowl, whisk together the miso, soy sauce, honey, butter, and rice vinegar until smooth.

3. Brush the salmon with the miso glaze. Place the fillets in the air fryer, leaving space between the fillets to ensure even cooking. Cook in batches if needed. Air-fry until the salmon begins to caramelize and flakes easily with a fork, 8 to 10 minutes.

4. Transfer the salmon to serving plates. Squeeze lime juice over the salmon and garnish with sesame seeds. Serve hot.

serving suggestion ★ I like to serve this in a bowl with rice and Not-Smashed Cucumber Salad (page 231) or Spicy Roasted Broccoli (page 244).

Makes 4 servings ★ Total time: about 15 minutes
Per serving ★ Calories: 360 ★ Protein: 41g ★ Carbohydrates: 13g ★ Fat: 16g

I love to stock up on frozen mahi-mahi fillets to keep on hand for a quick and easy meal. Mahi-mahi is a very lean white fish that pairs well with tropical fruit.

This recipe calls for blackening the fish using a blend of seasonings. For a shortcut, you can buy a pre-made jar of blackened seasoning mix, or you can make one yourself by adding a little bit of brown sugar to a dry rub of your choice (I use Swerve brown sugar erythritol instead of sugar). The trick with this recipe is to cook the fish at a lower heat, so you don't burn the seasonings but rather give them a nice dark color.

blackened mahi-mahi
with mango salsa

Mango Salsa

1 mango, finely diced

1 jalapeño, seeded and diced

¼ small red onion, finely diced

Juice of ½ lime

Pinch kosher salt

2 tablespoons chopped fresh cilantro

Mahi-Mahi

2 teaspoons kosher salt

1 teaspoon Swerve brown sugar erythritol

1 teaspoon paprika

1 teaspoon garlic powder

1 teaspoon onion powder

1 teaspoon chili powder

1 teaspoon dried parsley

4 (4-ounce) mahi-mahi fillets

2 tablespoons extra-virgin olive oil

1 tablespoon unsalted butter

1. Make the mango salsa: In a medium bowl, combine the mango, jalapeño, red onion, lime juice, salt, and cilantro. Toss to incorporate and set aside.

2. Make the blackened seasoning: In a small bowl, stir together the salt, Swerve, paprika, garlic powder, onion powder, chili powder, and parsley.

3. Cook the mahi-mahi: Pat the fillets dry with paper towels, then coat them in 1 tablespoon of olive oil and rub the blackened seasoning evenly over both sides of each fillet.

4. In a large skillet, heat the butter and the remaining 1 tablespoon of olive oil over medium heat. You want the pan hot, but not so hot that the sugar will instantly burn, so keep your eye on it and adjust the heat as needed.

5. Add the fish to the skillet and cook until opaque and dark golden brown on both sides, about 3 minutes per side. (Use a meat press, if you have one, for the best sear.) You'll know the fish is done when it's tender and flakes easily.

6. Serve the mahi-mahi hot, topped with the mango salsa.

serving suggestion ★ You can't go wrong pairing this dish with seasonal grilled or roasted vegetables, or a bit of rice.

Makes 4 servings ★ **Total time:** about 25 minutes
Per serving ★ **Calories:** 240 ★ **Protein:** 22g ★ **Carbohydrates:** 16g ★ **Fat:** 11g

This is another recipe that I keep frozen fish on hand to make—I look for bags of thick cuts of wild-caught cod at Target and Whole Foods. Fish tacos are incredibly slept-on in my opinion. They are so simple to make, quick to put together, and are a great high-protein option for a lunch or dinner. At restaurants, the fish is often deep-fried, but at home, I like to give the fish a flavorful rub and then bake and broil it. The simple slaw adds a nice crunch, and it comes together easily. In my opinion, it's essential to the taco, so don't skip it!

cod tacos
with simple slaw

Simple Slaw

3 cups coleslaw mix or finely shredded cabbage

2 tablespoons light mayonnaise

2 tablespoons seasoned rice vinegar

¼ cup chopped fresh cilantro

Juice of ½ lime

Kosher salt

Freshly ground black pepper

Cod Tacos

2 teaspoons Swerve brown sugar erythritol

2 teaspoons chile-lime seasoning

½ teaspoon chili powder

4 (6-ounce) cod fillets

1 tablespoon extra-virgin olive oil

8 corn tortillas

For Serving

Chopped fresh cilantro

Lime wedges

1. Preheat the oven to 450°F. Line a sheet pan with parchment paper.

2. Make the simple slaw: In a large bowl, combine the coleslaw mix, mayonnaise, rice vinegar, cilantro, and lime juice. Season with salt and pepper to taste and toss until well combined. Transfer to the fridge while cooking the cod.

3. Season the cod: In a small bowl, stir together the Swerve, chile-lime seasoning, and chili powder to make the seasoning rub. Coat the cod with the olive oil and season with the rub. Pat the seasoning to ensure it is sticking to the cod.

4. Place the cod on the prepared sheet pan and bake for 12 minutes. Then set the oven to broil and cook for an additional 2 minutes, or until the top is slightly caramelized and the fish flakes easily. Remove from the oven and set aside to cool.

5. While the cod is baking, heat the corn tortillas in a dry skillet or directly over a flame until warm and lightly charred. While still hot, wrap them in foil to steam for a few minutes before serving.

6. Assemble the tacos: Once the cod is cool enough to handle, break it into bite-size pieces. Top each tortilla with cod and slaw, and garnish with cilantro. Serve immediately, with lime wedges for squeezing on the side.

serving suggestion * Pair with a simple side salad, raw veggies with salsa or guacamole for dipping, or sliced avocado.

Makes 4 servings * **Total time:** about 30 minutes
Per serving * **Calories:** 300 * **Protein:** 29g * **Carbohydrates:** 28g * **Fat:** 8g

Inspired by a California roll, this bowl combines fresh jumbo crabmeat and a flavorful, spicy yogurt-mayo dressing to make a crab salad that's simple but feels fancy. If you don't have access to fresh crabmeat, canned or imitation crab will work, too. The freshness and bright flavors in this recipe makes it a delicious summertime lunch.

spicy crab roll in a bowl

Spicy Crab Salad

¼ cup whole-milk Greek yogurt

¼ cup light mayonnaise

¼ cup sriracha

1 teaspoon toasted sesame oil

1 pound lump crabmeat, picked over to remove any bits of shell, shredded

Rice Bowls

2 cups cooked white rice

2 tablespoons seasoned rice vinegar

1 cup Not-Smashed Cucumber Salad (page 231)

1 avocado, diced

4 green onions, sliced

Everything bagel seasoning

For Serving

Small nori (dried seaweed) sheets

serving suggestion ★ There are so many ways to customize these bowls! Try adding cooked shrimp, baked salmon, or diced roasted sweet potato. For a bowl with a lower glycemic index, you could use brown rice, cauliflower rice, or a base of salad greens.

1. Make the spicy crab salad: In a small bowl, whisk together the yogurt, mayo, sriracha, and sesame oil until well combined. Fold in the crabmeat until well incorporated and set aside.

2. Assemble the rice bowls: In a large bowl, mix together the cooked rice and rice vinegar until well combined. Scoop ½ cup of rice into each of 4 bowls. Dividing evenly, top with the Not-Smashed Cucumber Salad, avocado, green onions, everything bagel seasoning, and spicy crab salad. Serve with nori sheets on the side (you can either tear up the nori to sprinkle on top or use the whole sheets to pick up bites of the crab and rice).

tip: If you're using fresh crabmeat, make sure to check that there are no pieces of shell. There's nothing worse than biting into a piece of shell unexpectedly!

Makes 4 servings ★ **Total time:** about 15 minutes (if starting with cooked rice)
Per serving ★ **Calories:** 410 ★ **Protein:** 26g ★ **Carbohydrates:** 44g ★ **Fat:** 14g

I see shrimp boil mukbang videos on my For You Page all the time, and I was inspired to create an easier sheet-pan version of a shrimp boil. In my opinion, the ingredients typical in a shrimp boil—shrimp, spicy smoked sausages, corn, and spicy seasonings—taste even better when roasted in the oven. To go with it, I created a seasoned sauce that's like a thicker, more flavorful take on shrimp boil broth.

sheet-pan shrimp "boil"

Shrimp "Boil"

2 ears of corn, halved

1 (12-ounce) package andouille sausage, sliced into 1-inch rounds

1 pound large shell-on shrimp, deveined

Seafood Sauce

¼ cup unsalted butter

2 garlic cloves, minced

2 tablespoons chicken broth

1 teaspoon Old Bay seasoning

½ teaspoon Creole or Cajun seasoning

½ teaspoon lemon pepper seasoning

1 tablespoon chopped fresh parsley

For Serving

Lemon wedges

1. Preheat the oven to 425°F. Line a sheet pan with parchment paper.

2. **Prepare the shrimp "boil":** Set the corn on the prepared sheet pan and wrap tightly with foil. Bake for 20 minutes.

3. **Meanwhile, make the seafood sauce:** In a small saucepan, melt the butter over medium heat. Add the garlic and cook for 1 minute, until fragrant. Stir in the chicken broth, Old Bay, Creole seasoning, lemon pepper, and parsley. Set aside until the "boil" is ready.

4. Remove the sheet pan from the oven, take the corn out of the foil, and return it to the pan. Add the sausages to the sheet pan. Continue baking for 10 minutes.

5. Remove the sheet pan from the oven again and flip the sausages. Add the shrimp to the sheet pan and bake until the shrimp are opaque and the sausage is browned on both sides, 8 to 10 minutes.

6. To serve, toss the contents of the sheet pan in the seafood sauce. Serve hot, with lemon wedges for squeezing on the side.

serving suggestion ✶
I love to serve this dish with a jammy or hard-boiled egg (see page 45). The egg soaks up the spices in such a perfect way while not adding an overpowering flavor.

Makes 4 servings ✶ **Total time:** about 40 minutes
Per serving ✶ **Calories:** 370 ✶ **Protein:** 37g ✶ **Carbohydrates:** 13g ✶ **Fat:** 19g

This "tuna-cado"—tuna salad with avocado—was inspired by a recipe that shows up on my For You Page on social media all the time, a dupe of a popular sandwich from a place called Joe & the Juice. I've never even been to Joe & the Juice, but the fact that their tuna-cado still made its way to me was enough that I had to try it myself.

I substitute the mayonnaise in the tuna salad for cottage cheese, for more protein of course. There's still mayonnaise in the spicy pesto aioli, and I think that provides enough richness. (I find myself wanting to put this aioli on everything!)

As for the crispbread, I really like the brand Wasa, but any brand will do.

tuna-cado on crispbread
with spicy pesto aioli

Spicy Pesto Aioli

¼ cup store-bought pesto

2 teaspoons hot honey

¼ cup light mayonnaise

Tuna Salad

2 (5-ounce) cans tuna packed in olive oil

¼ cup whole-milk cottage cheese

2 tablespoons capers, drained

½ teaspoon dried dill

1 tablespoon fresh lemon juice

1½ teaspoons Dijon mustard

1 teaspoon soy sauce

¼ red onion, finely chopped

1 celery stalk, finely diced

For Serving

8 pieces multigrain crispbread, such as Wasa

1 large Hass avocado, thinly sliced

2 Roma tomatoes, thinly sliced

1 tablespoon chopped fresh dill (optional)

1 cup alfalfa sprouts (optional)

1. Make the spicy pesto aioli: In a small bowl, whisk together the pesto, hot honey, and mayonnaise until combined. Set aside.

2. Make the tuna salad: In a food processor, combine the tuna, cottage cheese, capers, dried dill, lemon juice, mustard, and soy sauce. Blend until combined.

3. Transfer the mixture to a large bowl. Add the red onion and celery and fold until evenly mixed.

4. To serve, spread a thin layer of aioli over each crispbread. Top each crispbread with a few slices of avocado, a generous spoonful of tuna salad, and 2 or 3 tomato slices. Garnish with fresh dill and alfalfa sprouts, if desired.

serving suggestion ✴ For an even lower-carb version of this dish, replace the crispbread with a cucumber! Halve a cucumber lengthwise, scoop out and discard the seeds, and pack the tuna mixture into the cucumber.

Makes 4 servings ✴ **Total time:** about 15 minutes
Per serving ✴ **Calories:** 400 ✴ **Protein:** 28g ✴ **Carbohydrates:** 34g ✴ **Fat:** 20g

tip: To roast poblanos without an air fryer, preheat your oven to 450°F, place the poblanos on a sheet pan lined with parchment paper, and roast for 20 to 25 minutes, turning halfway through, until the skins are charred and blistered. Alternatively, you can char poblanos directly over an open flame if you have a gas stove, using tongs to rotate until evenly blackened.

note: When working with scallops, remember to remove the side muscle before cooking. This tougher piece of muscle is edible, so it won't hurt you if you forget, but the texture is a bit chewy. You can find good-quality scallops in the freezer section of your local grocery store.

People are often intimidated to cook scallops at home. If that's you, I want you to know I've been in your shoes, and I get it—but once you get the hang of it, you can have restaurant-quality meals in the comfort of your home. When I was learning how to cook, I made scallops a lot, working on perfecting the sear. A good caramelization can really bring out the sweetness and flavor in the scallop.

Once you've nailed the sear, you'll find scallops go well with so many different flavors. I love them with this simple, creamy, blended sauce made with roasted peppers and Greek yogurt.

seared scallops
with creamy poblano sauce

Creamy Poblano Sauce

2 poblano chiles

½ cup whole-milk Greek yogurt

Juice of ½ lime

2 tablespoons heavy cream

Kosher salt

Scallops

1 pound large sea scallops, patted dry, side muscle removed

3 teaspoons extra-virgin olive oil

1 teaspoon garlic salt

2 tablespoons unsalted butter

For Serving

5 slices center cut bacon, cooked, then crumbled

½ cup store-bought crispy fried onions, crumbled

2 tablespoons chopped fresh cilantro

1. Roast the poblanos: Preheat the air fryer to 400°F. Place the poblanos in the air-fryer basket and roast for 15 to 17 minutes, turning halfway through, until the skins are charred and blistered (if you don't have an air fryer, see Tip). Remove the poblanos from the heat and immediately place them in a bowl. Cover the bowl tightly with plastic wrap to allow them to steam for 10 minutes. Then peel off the skins and remove the seeds.

2. Make the creamy poblano sauce: In a blender or food processor, combine the roasted poblanos, yogurt, lime juice, heavy cream, and a few pinches of salt. Blend until smooth and creamy. Taste and add more salt as desired.

3. Cook the scallops: In a large bowl, coat the scallops in 1½ teaspoons olive oil and season with garlic salt. In a large skillet, heat the butter and remaining 1½ teaspoons olive oil over medium-high heat until hot and shimmering. Working in batches if necessary, add the scallops in a single layer and sear until they develop a golden-brown crust on both sides, 2 to 3 minutes per side. Use a meat press if you have one. You can check if the scallops are cooked by pressing them with your finger. If they are taut but not hard, they are done. Remove the scallops from the skillet.

4. Spoon the creamy poblano sauce onto plates and top with the seared scallops. Top with crumbled bacon, fried onions, and cilantro and serve.

Makes 4 servings ★ **Total time:** about 40 minutes
Per serving ★ **Calories:** 320 ★ **Protein:** 20g ★ **Carbohydrates:** 12g ★ **Fat:** 21g

These crab cakes are a flavorful and elevated dish. They're served with a zesty cilantro-lime mayo that adds a tangy freshness to the rich crab and complements the green chiles beautifully. They're all my favorite things in a recipe: easy to make with sophisticated flavors.

I think the green chiles bring the perfect amount of heat, but you can up the spice in this dish by adding some fresh diced jalapeños as well.

green chile crab cakes

Cilantro-Lime Mayo

½ cup light mayonnaise

Juice of 1 lime

2 tablespoons finely chopped fresh cilantro

½ teaspoon kosher salt

Crab Cakes

3 tablespoons light mayonnaise

2 large eggs, lightly beaten

1 (4-ounce) can diced green chiles, drained

¼ cup minced fresh cilantro

1 teaspoon Old Bay seasoning

Kosher salt

Freshly ground black pepper

½ cup panko breadcrumbs

1 pound lump crabmeat, picked over to remove bits of shell

2 tablespoons extra-virgin olive oil

2 tablespoons salted butter

1. **Make the cilantro-lime mayo:** In a small bowl, combine the mayonnaise, lime juice, cilantro, salt, and 2 tablespoons of water. Mix until well combined. Store in the fridge until ready to serve.

2. **Make the crab cakes:** In a large bowl, combine the mayonnaise, eggs, green chiles, cilantro, and Old Bay. Add salt and pepper to taste. Mix gently to combine. Carefully fold in the panko and crabmeat until combined. Do not overmix or break up the crab.

3. Line a sheet pan with parchment paper. Divide the crab mixture into 8 equal portions and form into crab cakes, about 3 inches in diameter. Place the crab cakes on the prepared sheet pan and refrigerate for at least 30 minutes to help them firm up.

4. Set a large skillet over medium-high heat and add the olive oil and butter. Once the skillet is hot, add the crab cakes and cook until golden brown on both sides and opaque in the center, 2 to 3 minutes per side.

5. Serve the crab cakes with the cilantro-lime mayo.

tip: If you don't have breadcrumbs, throw some toasted bread or crackers into a blender or food processor with your favorite seasonings.

serving suggestion *

Serve with grilled corn on the cob (or sautéed corn), roasted vegetables, or a pickled slaw.

Makes 4 servings (8 crab cakes) * **Total time:** about 1 hour
Per serving * **Calories:** 390 * **Protein:** 24g * **Carbohydrates:** 15g * **Fat:** 25g

This simple sheet-pan dinner marries the bold, complex flavor profile of pesto with light, lean halibut (cod would work well here, too). You can find halibut in the freezer section of your local grocery store—I keep a bag on hand for a quick weeknight meal.

Using store-bought pesto makes this dish come together super-fast, in under 30 minutes—just be sure to choose a pesto made with good olive oil, one that you would happily eat on its own as a pasta sauce. That will make all the difference. This elevated dish makes a perfect afternoon lunch or summertime dinner.

sheet-pan pesto halibut
with asparagus

1 pound asparagus, woody ends snapped off

2 teaspoons extra-virgin olive oil

¼ teaspoon lemon pepper seasoning

¼ teaspoon garlic salt

4 (6-ounce) halibut fillets

Kosher salt

Freshly ground black pepper

¼ cup store-bought pesto (see headnote)

For Serving
Lemon wedges

1. Preheat the oven to 425°F. Line a sheet pan with parchment paper.

2. Place the asparagus on one side of the sheet pan, coat with the olive oil and sprinkle with lemon pepper seasoning and garlic salt. Place the halibut fillets on the other side of the sheet pan and season with salt and pepper. Spoon 1 tablespoon of pesto over each fillet and spread in an even layer. Bake until the halibut is opaque and flakes easily with a fork and the asparagus is tender, 12 to 14 minutes.

3. Transfer the halibut and asparagus to serving plates and serve with lemon wedges for squeezing on the side.

tip: I make this recipe in the oven, but you could also use the air fryer or grill. If using the air fryer, cook the halibut at 375°F for 8 to 10 minutes, depending on the thickness of the fillet. If grilling, brush the fish with oil to prevent sticking, then grill over medium-high heat for 3 to 4 minutes per side.

serving suggestion ★
Serve with a caprese salad, roasted or baked potatoes, or a quinoa pilaf or wild rice blend for a perfectly balanced dish.

Makes 4 servings ★ **Total time:** about 25 minutes
Per serving ★ **Calories:** 240 ★ **Protein:** 32g ★ **Carbohydrates:** 3g ★ **Fat:** 11g

I've been making this low-carb, high-protein recipe for years, and it's also one that went viral on social media. With cream cheese and a sprinkle of everything bagel seasoning, this recipe splits the difference between a sushi roll and a bagel with lox. And you can have the whole thing ready in minutes, since no cooking is required.

If you're gluten-free, you can easily swap the soy sauce for tamari.

salmon–cucumber roll–ups

1 large English cucumber

¼ cup cream cheese, at room temperature

Everything bagel seasoning

4 ounces thinly sliced smoked salmon

¼ avocado, thinly sliced

For Serving

1 tablespoon sesame seeds

1 teaspoon sliced chives (optional)

Soy sauce

Pickled ginger

Wasabi

1. Using a mandolin or a Y-shaped vegetable peeler, slice the cucumber lengthwise to create thin, wide ribbons.

2. Lay all of the cucumber slices flat, arranging them vertically and slightly overlapping with each other to create a large rectangle. Pat them dry with paper towels. Spread a thin layer of the cream cheese on the end of the rectangle closer to you, covering about one-third of the cucumbers. Sprinkle everything bagel seasoning all over the cream cheese, then top with smoked salmon and avocado slices.

3. Starting from the cream cheese–covered end, carefully roll up the cucumber base ribbon tightly around the filling, creating a log. Slice into ¾-inch pieces.

4. Arrange the rolls on a serving platter. Garnish with sesame seeds and chives (if using), and serve with soy sauce, pickled ginger, and wasabi on the side.

serving suggestion ✷ To make this a full meal, serve with some white or brown rice.

Makes 1 roll (8 to 10 pieces, cut) ✷ **Total time:** about 15 minutes

Per roll ✷ **Calories:** 470 ✷ **Protein:** 30g ✷ **Carbohydrates:** 14g ✷ **Fat:** 34g

pork

I love the depth of flavor that you can achieve from slow-cooking—and this dish is no exception. This is a great make-ahead recipe—you can throw the ingredients in the slow cooker in the morning to serve that evening. Or make it on the weekend as meal prep for the week. In any case, plan for a long cooking time. The slow-cooking process allows the fat to render slowly, so the meat cooks in its own fat.

slow-cooker bbq pulled pork

1 tablespoon Swerve brown sugar erythritol

1 tablespoon garlic powder

1 tablespoon onion powder

1 tablespoon ancho chile powder

1 tablespoon smoked paprika

¼ teaspoon cayenne pepper

2 teaspoons kosher salt, plus more for seasoning

½ teaspoon freshly ground black pepper, plus more for seasoning

4 pounds boneless pork shoulder (see Tip)

1 tablespoon extra-virgin olive oil

1 cup sugar-free BBQ sauce

tip: When choosing your pork shoulder, you can get one with a bone—if you do, just make sure you cook it a bit longer, so the bone pulls out of the meat easily.

1. **Make the spice rub:** In a small bowl, combine the Swerve, garlic powder, onion powder, chile powder, smoked paprika, cayenne, salt, and pepper.

2. Coat the pork shoulder in olive oil and season heavily all over with salt and pepper. Season the meat with the spice rub, pressing the meat to ensure the spices adhere.

3. Place the pork in the slow cooker fat-side up. Cover and cook on low for 8 to 10 hours, or on high for 4 to 6 hours. You'll know the pork is done when it's tender and easily pulls apart with a fork. Cooking time will vary based on the size of the pork shoulder.

4. Set your oven to broil and allow it to preheat for 5 minutes.

5. Carefully remove the pork shoulder from the slow cooker. Use two forks to shred the meat. Transfer the shredded pork to a large sheet pan and pour any reserved liquid from the slow cooker on top. Transfer the sheet pan to the oven and broil the shredded pork for 4 to 5 minutes, or until the edges get crispy. Toss in the BBQ sauce and enjoy.

note: To make Simple Pulled Pork, skip the BBQ sauce—then you can use the meat as carnitas and serve it on tacos, topped with red onions, avocado slices, and your favorite salsa. Or serve over lettuce with pickled vegetables, carrots, red cabbage, and cucumbers to make a banh mi–inspired bowl (add a dipping sauce made from fish sauce, lime juice, garlic, and sugar).

Makes 12 servings * Total time: about 8 hours 15 minutes
Per serving * Calories: 350 * Protein: 27g * Carbohydrates: 9g * Fat: 23g

This is, hands down, my favorite pork tenderloin recipe. The balsamic vinegar caramelizes on the meat, adding a touch of sweetness, and the herby spice rub creates a really flavorful crust. If you're meal prepping for the week or want to serve this for guests, you can double the recipe and make two tenderloins at once—the cooking time won't change. This same seasoning rub is also delicious on grilled pork chops.

balsamic & herb–roasted pork tenderloin

¼ teaspoon rubbed sage

¼ teaspoon dry ground mustard

½ teaspoon dried thyme

1 teaspoon kosher salt

½ teaspoon freshly ground black pepper

1 pound pork tenderloin

1 tablespoon extra-virgin olive oil

1 tablespoon balsamic vinegar

1. Preheat the oven to 425°F. Line a sheet pan with parchment paper.

2. Make the spice rub: In a small bowl, combine the sage, ground mustard, thyme, salt, and pepper.

3. Rub the pork tenderloin with the olive oil and balsamic vinegar. Then season it all over with the spice mixture. If possible, let rest it for 30 minutes to help the flavors penetrate into the meat.

4. Set the pork on the prepared baking sheet. Transfer to the oven and roast until the internal temperature of the pork tenderloin reaches 145°F, 20 to 25 minutes. Then set the oven to broil and cook the pork for 1 to 2 minutes, until it has a good browning on top.

5. Let the pork tenderloin rest for 5 minutes to lock in the juices, then slice and serve.

note: If you can spare the time, allow the pork to marinate with the spices for at least 30 minutes before cooking. The salt will work to tenderize the meat.

tip: I make this recipe in the oven, but it also works in the air fryer. To air-fry, cut the tenderloin in half before seasoning to ensure it cooks evenly (and fits in the air-fryer basket). Preheat the air fryer to 400°F, then cook the pork for about 25 minutes, flipping halfway through, until the internal temperature reaches 145°F. Let it rest for 5 minutes before slicing and serving.

Makes 4 servings ★ Total time: about 25 minutes, plus 30 minutes marinating time
Per serving ★ Calories: 160 ★ **Protein:** 25g ★ **Carbohydrates:** 1g ★ **Fat:** 6g

serving suggestion ★
Pair the tenderloin with Garlic Cauliflower Mash (page 232) or Balsamic Brussels Sprouts (page 239) for a delicious, elevated weeknight meal.

This loaded sausage recipe was a huge hit on social media—it's one of my most viral recipes to date. It totally satisfies the craving for those Italian sausage sandwiches with hot peppers and cheese (except it ditches the bread).

This dish doesn't take long to cook, but time and patience are still essential. You have to cook the sausages slowly at a lower heat than you'd expect, which keeps them from curling as they cook and leaves you with a nice browned crust.

I think the key to success in this recipe is in butterflying the sausages lengthwise, which gives you a flat surface that browns nicely—a great base to smother in balsamic-glazed peppers and onions and plenty of mozzarella.

loaded italian sausages

5 sweet or spicy Italian sausages

1 tablespoon extra-virgin olive oil

2 red or green bell peppers, finely diced

1 yellow onion, finely diced

Kosher salt

Freshly ground black pepper

1 tablespoon balsamic vinegar

1 cup shredded mozzarella cheese

¼ cup Chicago-style giardiniera

tip: Be sure to look for spicy Chicago-style giardiniera, an Italian pickled vegetable relish that is a must for Italian beef or sausages.

serving suggestion *
Serve with a simple side salad for the perfect summertime dinner.

1. Remove the sausages from the fridge 30 minutes prior to cooking.

2. Preheat the oven to 375°F. Line a sheet pan with parchment paper (or use a 9 by 13-inch baking dish).

3. Using a sharp knife, butterfly the Italian sausages: Slice them lengthwise, but don't cut all the way through. Bend them open and use the back of the knife to help flatten them, creating a larger cooking surface.

4. Set a large skillet over medium-low heat and add the olive oil. Once the olive oil is hot, place the sausages cut-sides down in the skillet. Don't stir—let them brown in the pan for 4 to 5 minutes, until a nice crust forms. Transfer the sausages to the prepared sheet pan or baking dish, cut-sides up. Set aside.

5. Add the bell peppers and onion to the same skillet and adjust the heat to medium-high. Sauté until the vegetables are tender, 5 to 6 minutes. Season with salt and black pepper, then add the balsamic vinegar and continue to cook for 1 to 2 minutes, stirring often, until the balsamic coats the vegetables like a glaze.

6. Use tongs to distribute the sautéed bell peppers and onions evenly on top of the sausages. Spread the mozzarella and giardiniera over the vegetables.

7. Transfer the sheet pan or baking dish to the oven and roast until the cheese is melted and bubbling, 10 to 12 minutes. Let the sausages cool for a few minutes before serving.

Makes 5 servings * **Total time:** about 1 hour 10 minutes
Per serving * **Calories:** 310 * **Protein:** 21g * **Carbohydrates:** 8g * **Fat:** 21g

What is it about grandmothers and their cooking? For me, my grandma's recipes make the best comfort food, probably because each bite of food takes me back to a specific moment with her. When my grandma visited us when I was a kid, I always asked her to cook "confetti" pork chops—the "confetti" being colorful diced sautéed veggies.

In this recipe, the pork is baked low and slow, keeping it moist and tender, topped with vegetable "confetti" and Campbell's cream of mushroom soup. And no, you can't use a different brand—it has to be Campbell's. This is Grandma's recipe, after all!

grandma's confetti pork chops

2 tablespoons extra-virgin olive oil

1 yellow bell pepper, finely diced

1 red onion, finely diced

2 celery stalks, finely diced

2 large carrots, finely diced

½ teaspoon garlic salt

2 pounds boneless pork chops (about 5 pork chops), sliced ½ inch thick

Kosher salt

Freshly ground black pepper

2 tablespoons white wine vinegar

1 (10.5-ounce) can Campbell's condensed cream of mushroom soup

serving suggestion * To balance out the richness of this dish, serve with a light salad of romaine, mini cucumbers, and sliced avocado, tossed with a bit of salt, pepper, olive oil, and vinegar.

1. Preheat the oven to 350°F.

2. Make the vegetable "confetti": In a large skillet, heat 1 tablespoon of the olive oil over medium heat. Add the bell pepper, onion, celery, and carrots and sauté until tender, 8 to 10 minutes. Season with garlic salt, transfer to a plate, and set aside. Hold onto the skillet; you'll use it again in a minute.

3. Season the pork chops on both sides with salt and pepper. In the same skillet, heat the remaining 1 tablespoon olive oil over medium heat. Add the pork chops and cook until nicely browned on both sides, about 3 minutes per side. If they don't look done yet, that's okay—the pork chops will finish cooking in the oven.

4. Transfer the pork chops to a 9 by 13-inch baking dish.

5. Add the white wine vinegar to the skillet and use a wooden spoon to deglaze it, scraping up any browned bits from the bottom of the pan. Return the sautéed vegetables to the skillet and stir to incorporate. Then add the can of cream of mushroom soup and stir to combine.

6. Pour the vegetable-soup mixture over the pork chops in the baking dish, ensuring the pork chops are fully covered.

7. Cover the baking dish with aluminum foil. Bake until the pork chops are fork-tender, about 1½ hours. Serve hot.

Makes 5 servings * **Total time:** about 2 hours
Per serving * **Calories:** 340 * **Protein:** 35g * **Carbohydrates:** 12g * **Fat:** 17g

I love egg rolls as much as the next person, but they're a ton of work to make at home. That's why I came up with this one-pan dish, with forkfuls of delicious vegetables, ground pork, and the classic egg roll seasonings. You might think you'll miss the fried, crispy wonton wrapper, but honestly, this dish is so good I think you'll forget about it. I meal prep this dish often because it gets better and better in the fridge.

Coconut aminos add a touch of sweetness to the pork and also help it caramelize. If you like a little more heat, add sriracha or up the garlic chili oil. Instead of the coleslaw mix, you can also use finely sliced cabbage, kale, or Brussels sprouts. You can also swap the pork for the same amount of beef.

egg roll in a bowl

1 pound ground pork

4 green onions, chopped, whites and greens separated

4 garlic cloves, minced

1 teaspoon minced fresh ginger

1 teaspoon garlic chili oil, plus more to taste

1 (28-ounce) bag coleslaw mix (or ½ large head cabbage, shredded)

⅓ cup coconut aminos

1 teaspoon toasted sesame oil

1. Set a large skillet or wok over medium-high heat. Add the ground pork and cook until browned, using a spatula to break up any large pieces, 5 to 7 minutes.

2. Add the white parts of the green onion, the garlic, ginger, and garlic chili oil to the skillet and cook for 1 to 2 minutes, stirring often, until fragrant. Add the coleslaw mix and stir to incorporate. Cook, stirring frequently, until the vegetables are tender, 5 to 7 minutes.

3. Add in the coconut aminos and sesame oil and stir well to coat all the ingredients. Cook for an additional 2 to 3 minutes, until all the liquid is absorbed.

4. Serve hot, garnished with the green ends of the green onions.

Makes 4 servings * **Total time:** about 25 minutes
Per serving * **Calories:** 340 * **Protein:** 23g * **Carbohydrates:** 24g * **Fat:** 18g

Did you think it was possible to cook a full rack of ribs in just 40 minutes? I'm still surprised by how great this air-fryer recipe turns out. These ribs come out with a beautiful caramelized crust, thanks to the Asian-inspired ginger-garlic marinade and the searing convection heat of the air fryer. It's a nontraditional but very efficient and effective way to cook ribs—and a great way to do meal prep as well.

This recipe is a great option if you're hosting a party and need to move fast and get lots of dishes cooked quickly, and especially if your oven or grill is in use for something else.

air-fryer ginger-garlic ribs

2 pounds baby back ribs

⅔ cup coconut aminos

2 tablespoons Swerve brown sugar erythritol

3 garlic cloves, minced

1 teaspoon minced fresh ginger

1 teaspoon kosher salt

½ teaspoon freshly ground black pepper

¼ cup Bachan's Original Japanese Barbecue Sauce, or other teriyaki-style sauce of your choice, plus more for serving

1. Use sturdy kitchen shears to cut the ribs into 4 sections to fit in your air fryer, cutting along the bone.

2. Make the marinade: In a large bowl, combine the coconut aminos, Swerve, garlic, ginger, salt, and pepper and mix well. Add the sectioned ribs to the marinade, and toss them to ensure they are well coated. Cover and refrigerate for at least 1 hour, but preferably overnight for maximum flavor.

3. Preheat the air fryer to 350°F.

4. Remove the ribs from the marinade and allow any excess marinade to drip off. Place the ribs in a single layer in the air-fryer basket. Air-fry for 30 minutes, flipping halfway through to ensure even cooking.

5. Remove the ribs from the air fryer and brush them generously with the Japanese BBQ sauce. Then return the ribs to the air fryer and cook for an additional 5 minutes to allow the sauce to set and caramelize slightly.

6. Let the ribs rest for a few minutes, then serve hot, with more Japanese BBQ sauce on the side.

tip: If you have leftovers, save some rib meat to add to the Egg Roll in a Bowl (page 202)!

serving suggestion ✶
Serve with Not-Smashed Cucumber Salad (page 231).

Makes 4 servings ✶ Total time: about 50 minutes, plus 1 hour marinating time
Per serving ✶ Calories: 560 ✶ **Protein:** 40g ✶ **Carbohydrates:** 25g ✶ **Fat:** 34g

I love when I create a recipe, omit an ingredient (in this case, bread), and find I don't even miss it. I saw grinder sub sandwiches going viral on social media, and I thought, why not create a grinder sub salad? Ham, turkey, salami, and mozzarella make this salad rich and protein-packed, and hot peppers, onions, and tomatoes provide spice and freshness.

I think the secret to this recipe is the tangy, creamy mayo-based dressing, which is seasoned with oregano to emulate the classic sub sandwich flavor. I sometimes add chickpeas for a little extra protein and bite.

grinder sub salad

Dressing

3 tablespoons light mayonnaise

2 tablespoons red wine vinegar

Pinch dried oregano

Kosher salt

Freshly ground black pepper

Salad

½ head iceberg lettuce, shredded

1 (4-ounce) package thinly sliced pepperoni

¼ pound thinly sliced salami

¼ pound sliced deli ham, finely chopped

¼ pound sliced deli turkey, finely chopped

1 cup shredded mozzarella cheese

½ cup sliced pickled hot cherry peppers

¼ small red onion, thinly sliced

1 cup halved cherry tomatoes

1. Make the dressing: In a small bowl, combine the mayonnaise and red wine vinegar and stir until smooth and creamy. Add the oregano and salt and pepper to taste. Mix until fully incorporated. Taste and adjust the seasoning if needed. Set aside.

2. Assemble the salad: On a large platter or in a salad bowl, arrange a base of shredded lettuce. Layer the pepperoni, salami, and deli meats on top of the lettuce, either in sections or mixed together. Scatter the mozzarella, cherry peppers, red onion, and tomatoes on top.

3. Drizzle the dressing evenly across the salad. Gently toss the salad so the dressing evenly coats the ingredients. Serve immediately.

tip: I originally made this salad in a mason jar, which you could do to make a to-go salad or for meal prep. Add the dressing just before serving and shake the jar to toss.

Makes 4 servings * **Total time:** about 15 minutes
Per serving * **Calories:** 390 * **Protein:** 27g * **Carbohydrates:** 10g * **Fat:** 27g

Cooking a giant slab of ribs might seem intimidating, but this hands-off, low-and-slow oven version will get you past that fear and give you delicious, fall-off-the-bone ribs. I struggled for years with making ribs on the smoker, but once I discovered this oven method, it got so much easier (and juicier!)—plus, I loved that I could have this summertime treat year-round. These ribs aren't actually smoked, but a flavorful dry rub with smoked paprika and ancho chile powder still gives them a nice smoky flavor.

The key to getting a nice, almost-caramelized crust is to let the seasoned ribs rest at room temperature before you cook. This allows the seasoning to be absorbed on both sides. I prefer to use Swerve brown sugar erythritol in my dry rub blends—I still get the sweetness of brown sugar, but without the carbs.

oven–baked bbq baby back ribs

½ tablespoon Swerve brown sugar erythritol

½ tablespoon smoked paprika

½ tablespoon ancho chile powder

½ tablespoon onion powder

½ tablespoon garlic powder

1 teaspoon kosher salt

½ teaspoon freshly ground black pepper

¼ teaspoon cayenne pepper

1 rack baby back ribs

1 tablespoon extra-virgin olive oil

2 tablespoons salted butter, cut into ½-tablespoon knobs

2 tablespoons honey

½ cup sugar-free BBQ sauce

1. **Make the spice rub:** In a small bowl, stir together the Swerve, smoked paprika, chile powder, onion powder, garlic powder, salt, black pepper, and cayenne. Set aside.

2. **Prep the ribs:** Remove the membrane from the back of the ribs by sliding a table knife under the membrane on a bone in the center of the rack. Separate the membrane all the way to the end of the bone; then pull upward on the membrane with a paper towel on each side to lift the membrane off of the ribs.

3. Preheat the oven to 275°F. Line a sheet pan with parchment paper.

4. Rub the olive oil on both sides of the ribs. Generously season one side of the ribs with the spice rub, pressing it into the meat to ensure the seasoning adheres to the ribs.

5. Lay a large sheet of heavy-duty aluminum foil on a flat surface. Add the butter and honey to the center, then place the ribs meat-side down on top. Wrap the ribs tightly in the foil, ensuring there are no leaks. Place the wrapped ribs on the prepared sheet pan.

(recipe continues)

Makes 4 servings * Total time: about 4 hours
Per serving * Calories: 520 * Protein: 31g * Carbohydrates: 18g * Fat: 38g

serving suggestion ★ Ribs
pair well with Simple Slaw
(page 177), loaded baked
potatoes (or loaded broccoli), or
Bacon & Jalapeño Deviled Eggs
(page 36).

6. Bake the ribs for 3 hours, then remove the ribs from the oven and set the oven on broil.

7. Carefully remove the ribs from the foil and put them back on the sheet pan, keeping them meat-side down.

8. Return the sheet pan to the oven. Broil the ribs for 4 to 5 minutes on each side. They should be well-browned, but keep an eye on them so they don't burn. Remove the ribs from the oven and generously brush them with BBQ sauce.

9. Let the ribs rest for 5 minutes to allow the ribs to absorb the BBQ sauce. Slice and serve with extra BBQ sauce on the side.

It never occurred to me that you could make breakfast sausage—I used to always buy it. But now that I've figured out how to make my own, I'll never go back. It's so quick, and best of all, you can control the seasoning. I like mine with a healthy dose of onion and garlic, a bit lighter on the dried herbs, and with a touch of maple syrup, which also helps it brown as it cooks.

I often use these sausages for my Sweet & Spicy Breakfast Sandwiches (page 41), and they also freeze beautifully, either cooked or uncooked, making them a great staple for a quick breakfast.

simple breakfast sausage

1 pound ground pork

2 tablespoons maple syrup

1 teaspoon seasoned salt

½ teaspoon freshly ground black pepper

1 teaspoon garlic powder

1 teaspoon onion powder

½ teaspoon dried sage

¼ teaspoon dried thyme

¼ teaspoon cayenne pepper

serving suggestion *
Serve with Maple Cinnamon Pancakes (page 53) or toast and Jammy Eggs (page 45).

storage
* Store uncooked patties in the fridge for up to 3 days or freeze for up to 2 months. To freeze, wrap the sausage patties in parchment or wax paper and store in a single layer in a freezer-safe container or resealable ziplock bag.

* To serve, remove from the freezer and place in the fridge overnight to thaw before cooking.

1. In a large bowl, combine the ground pork with the maple syrup, seasoned salt, black pepper, garlic powder, onion powder, sage, thyme, and cayenne. Using clean hands, mix the ingredients together until well combined.

2. Divide the mixture into 8 equal portions. Form each portion into a patty about 2 inches in diameter and ½ inch thick. If storing, you can freeze the patties at this point and have them ready for whenever you need them (see Storage).

3. To cook the patties, line a plate with paper towels and set it near the stovetop. Set a large skillet or cast-iron pan over medium heat. Once the skillet is hot, add the sausage patties in a single layer, working in batches to avoid overcrowding the pan. Cook until the patties are well-browned on both sides, 2 to 3 minutes per side. Transfer the sausage patties to the paper towels to drain any excess grease. Serve hot.

tip: Feel free to use a sugar-free maple syrup to lower the sugar levels. You can also substitute ground turkey or chicken for the pork if you'd like.

Makes 8 sausage patties * **Total time:** about 20 minutes
Per sausage patty * **Calories:** 130 * **Protein:** 10g * **Carbohydrates:** 4g * **Fat:** 8g

People don't realize how easy it is to cook pork belly. You might think you have to leave it to the professionals, but honestly, it's basically like cooking extra-thick bacon. I like to cook it in the air fryer—I get perfect results every time. Marinating the pork belly overnight with a bit of sweetener (in this case, honey) helps it get crispy and caramelized when it cooks. If you don't have coconut aminos, you can use soy sauce; just add a little extra honey for the sweetness that the coconut aminos provide. I think this pork belly tastes best wrapped in fresh, cold, crisp lettuce, but you could also serve it on its own or with rice.

air-fryer pork belly lettuce wraps

Pork Belly

¼ cup coconut aminos

1 tablespoon sriracha

1½ teaspoons honey

1 teaspoon toasted sesame oil

2 garlic cloves, minced

1 teaspoon minced fresh ginger

1 pound skin-off pork belly, cut into ½-inch cubes

For Serving

1 head butter or romaine lettuce

2 green onions, thinly sliced

1 teaspoon sesame seeds

1. Make the marinade: In a large bowl, stir together the coconut aminos, sriracha, honey, sesame oil, garlic, and ginger. Add the sliced pork belly and toss to coat evenly.

2. Cover the bowl and allow the pork belly to marinate in the fridge for at least 30 minutes, but preferably overnight for maximum flavor.

3. Preheat the air fryer to 400°F.

4. Remove the pork belly from the marinade, allowing any excess marinade to drip off. Arrange the pork belly in a single layer in the air-fryer basket. Cook in batches if needed. Air-fry for 15 to 20 minutes, flipping every 5 minutes, until golden brown and crispy.

5. While the pork belly is cooking, separate the head of lettuce into individual leaves, washing and drying as many as you'll need for serving.

6. Remove the pork belly from the air fryer and let rest for a few minutes.

7. To serve, place a heaping spoonful of pork belly in each lettuce leaf. Garnish with green onions and sesame seeds.

serving suggestion *
Serve with Not-Smashed Cucumber Salad (page 231) and Stir-Fried Cabbage (page 235).

Makes 4 servings * **Total time:** about 1 hour
Per serving * **Calories:** 250 * **Protein:** 15g * **Carbohydrates:** 8g * **Fat:** 17g

These pork skewers are absolutely delicious and packed with flavor, thanks to a decadent garlic-Parmesan sauce. You can use whatever cut of pork you prefer, but I personally love a tenderloin for these skewers. I used to make these in the air fryer, but once I tried them on the grill, there was no going back.

grilled garlic-parmesan pork skewers

2 tablespoons extra-virgin olive oil

1 teaspoon garlic powder

1 teaspoon onion powder

1 teaspoon dried parsley

1 teaspoon paprika

2 teaspoons garlic salt

½ teaspoon freshly ground black pepper

2 pounds pork tenderloin, cut into 1-inch cubes

Neutral oil, for grill

Garlic-Parmesan Sauce

¼ cup unsalted butter

½ cup grated Parmesan cheese

1 teaspoon garlic salt

1 teaspoon dried parsley

1. If using wooden skewers, soak them in water for at least 30 minutes before grilling to prevent burning.

2. In a large bowl, combine the olive oil, garlic powder, onion powder, parsley, paprika, garlic salt, and pepper. Add the cubed pork and toss until the pork is evenly coated. Thread the pork onto the skewers, ensuring each skewer is evenly filled.

3. Preheat the grill to medium-high and oil the grates.

4. Place the pork skewers on the grill and cook, turning occasionally, until pork is cooked through and has a nice char on the outside, 10 to 12 minutes.

5. Meanwhile, make the garlic-Parmesan sauce: In a small saucepan, melt the butter over medium heat. Stir in the Parmesan, garlic salt, and parsley and mix until the cheese is fully incorporated and the sauce is smooth. Remove from the heat and set aside.

6. Remove the pork skewers from the grill and transfer to a serving platter. Using a brush or spoon, generously coat the pork skewers with the garlic-Parmesan sauce. Serve immediately.

serving suggestion *
Serve with Pesto-Parmesan Green Beans (page 243) and Spanish yellow rice.

Makes 8 servings * **Total time:** about 30 minutes
Per serving * **Calories:** 230 * **Protein:** 26g * **Carbohydrates:** 2g * **Fat:** 13g

If you have a busy weekend ahead of you, or if you can already tell you won't want to cook in your downtime this week, this dish is a great choice—it makes enough to feed a family of four for a solid couple of days. This recipe cooks slowly using a Dutch oven, allowing the pork loin to get more and more tender as it's cooked. Simmered in a bright salsa verde that balances out the richness of the pork, this super-comforting stew will keep you satisfied all week. You can try your hand at making salsa verde if you'd like, but I just use my favorite jarred version.

pork chile verde stew

2 tablespoons extra-virgin olive oil

3 pounds pork loin, cut into 1-inch cubes

1 medium onion, chopped

4 garlic cloves, minced

¼ teaspoon ground cumin

2 (16-ounce) jars store-bought salsa verde

½ cup chicken broth

1 teaspoon kosher salt

½ teaspoon freshly ground black pepper

2 tablespoons heavy cream

For Serving

Sour cream

¼ cup chopped fresh cilantro

Pickled red onions

1. Preheat the oven to 350°F.

2. Set a Dutch oven over medium-high heat and add the olive oil. Once the oil is hot, add the cubed pork and sear until all sides are browned, 8 to 10 minutes.

3. Add the onion to the Dutch oven and sauté until softened, 4 to 5 minutes, stirring frequently. Add the garlic and cumin and sauté for 1 minute, until fragrant.

4. Pour the salsa verde and chicken broth over the pork to coat it. Season with the salt and pepper. Cover the Dutch oven with the lid and transfer to the oven.

5. Cook the stew until the pork is very tender, about 2 hours. Remove the stew from the oven, add the heavy cream, and stir to incorporate.

6. Serve the stew with a dollop of sour cream and garnish with cilantro and pickled red onions.

serving suggestion * Enjoy as a rice bowl, garnished with pickled red onions and a dollop of Greek yogurt or sour cream.

Makes 12 servings * **Total time:** about 2 hours 45 minutes
Per serving * **Calories:** 250 * **Protein:** 20g * **Carbohydrates:** 7g * **Fat:** 14g

These skewers are inspired by al pastor tacos, which strike the perfect balance of spicy, savory, and sweet. If you've never had tacos al pastor, I highly suggest ordering them next time you're at a taco shop. Marinated pork and sweet pineapple (my favorite part) are stacked and grilled on a vertical spit, then shaved off in thin slices and served piping hot. Far from making your own giant spit of al pastor meat (I wish!), you can cook skewers on a grill to achieve a similar flavor.

This recipe calls for pork tenderloin, but you could also use pork chops. This makes a fantastic summertime dinner or a dish to serve at a BBQ with friends.

grilled pork skewers, al pastor style

2 whole chipotle peppers in adobo sauce

1 tablespoon extra-virgin olive oil

¼ cup pineapple juice

½ tablespoon honey

Juice of ½ lime

1 teaspoon kosher salt

½ teaspoon freshly ground black pepper

1 pound pork tenderloin, cut into 1-inch cubes

1 cup fresh pineapple, cut into 1-inch cubes

1 red onion, cut into 1-inch pieces

½ cup sugar-free BBQ sauce

Neutral oil, for grill

1. **Make the marinade:** In a blender, combine the chipotle peppers, olive oil, pineapple juice, honey, lime juice, salt, and black pepper. Blend until smooth.

2. **Marinate the pork:** Place the pork cubes in a large bowl or resealable ziplock bag. Pour the marinade over the pork and toss to coat evenly. Cover and refrigerate for at least 2 hours or up to overnight.

3. If using wooden skewers, soak them in water for at least 30 minutes before grilling to prevent burning.

4. Thread the marinated pork, pineapple, and red onion onto the skewers, alternating the ingredients.

5. Preheat the grill to medium-high heat and oil the grates.

6. Place the skewers on the grates and grill, turning occasionally, until the pork is cooked through and has a nice char on the outside, about 20 minutes (it should have an internal temperature of at least 145°F). Remove the skewers from the grill and brush with BBQ sauce. Let them rest for a few minutes before serving.

serving suggestion * The skewers pair nicely with white rice or Garlic-Herb Cauliflower Rice (page 236). It's also great served over tortilla chips, nachos-style.

Makes 4 servings * **Total time:** about 30 minutes, plus 2 hours marinating time
Per serving * **Calories:** 270 * **Protein:** 26g * **Carbohydrates:** 28g * **Fat:** 6g

The key to this dish lies in the spice rub, which includes Swerve brown sugar erythritol to help caramelize the pork, creating a restaurant-quality crust. (You can also use regular brown sugar or any other sweetener you have on hand.) These simple but delicious pork chops would be outstanding made on the grill as well.

Much like the Oven-Baked BBQ Baby Back Ribs (page 209), this is a method you can scale up or down without adding cooking time, so feel free to double it for a larger crowd. I've calculated the macros based on a 5-ounce serving of meat (about 6 ounces before cooking).

air-fryer pork chops

1 tablespoon Swerve brown sugar erythritol

1 teaspoon garlic powder

1 teaspoon paprika

½ teaspoon kosher salt

½ teaspoon freshly ground black pepper

4 boneless pork chops, 1½ to 2 inches thick

Olive oil cooking spray

1. Preheat the air fryer to 400°F for about 5 minutes.

2. Make the spice rub: In a small bowl, combine the Swerve, garlic powder, paprika, salt, and black pepper.

3. Pat the pork chops dry with paper towels. Sprinkle the spice rub evenly over both sides of the pork chops, pressing it gently into the meat to ensure it adheres.

4. Lightly coat the inside of the air-fryer basket with cooking spray to prevent sticking. Place the seasoned pork chops in a single layer in the air-fryer basket. Depending on the size of your air fryer, you may need to cook in batches.

5. Air-fry until the pork chops reach an internal temperature of 145°F and are golden brown on the outside, 12 to 15 minutes, flipping halfway through.

6. Remove the pork chops from the air fryer and let them rest for 3 to 5 minutes to keep them tender and juicy. Serve hot.

serving suggestion ✳ Pair these simple pork chops with a veggie side like Pesto-Parmesan Green Beans (page 243), Garlic Cauliflower Mash (page 232), Honey Butter–Glazed Carrots (page 240), or Stir-Fried Cabbage (page 235).

Makes 4 servings ✳ **Total time:** about 20 minutes
Per serving ✳ **Calories:** 240 ✳ **Protein:** 32g ✳ **Carbohydrates:** 4g ✳ **Fat:** 11g

There are lots of great ways to season pork chops, but the Italian seasoning and the lemony garlic butter in this dish is one of my favorites! Together, the lemon and garlic butter create such a rich but bright and super-flavorful sauce. Though it's quick and easy to put together—only 20 minutes of hands-on activity— you should leave time for the pork to rest after adding the seasonings. I also recommend building in some time to allow the pork to come to room temperature before you begin cooking.

lemony garlic butter pork chops

1 tablespoon Italian seasoning

2 teaspoons lemon pepper seasoning

1 teaspoon garlic powder

2 teaspoons kosher salt

1 teaspoon freshly ground black pepper

4 (6-ounce) boneless pork chops

2 tablespoons extra-virgin olive oil

2 tablespoons unsalted butter

2 garlic cloves, minced

¼ cup fresh lemon juice (about 2 lemons)

1. Make the seasoning blend: In a small bowl, combine the Italian seasoning, lemon pepper seasoning, garlic powder, salt, and black pepper.

2. Pat the pork chops dry with paper towels. Coat them with 1 tablespoon of the olive oil and sprinkle the seasoning blend evenly over both sides, pressing it into the meat gently to ensure it adheres. (Leftover seasoning blend can be stored indefinitely.)

3. In a large skillet, heat the remaining 1 tablespoon olive oil over medium-high heat. Once the oil is hot, add the pork chops and sear until they develop a golden-brown crust on both sides, 4 to 5 minutes per side. Use a meat press if you have one.

4. Reduce the heat to medium-low and add the butter and garlic to the skillet with the pork chops. Once the butter is melted and the garlic is fragrant, add the lemon juice. Tilt the skillet slightly, and use a spoon to baste the pork chops with the lemony garlic butter sauce.

5. Transfer the pork chops to a plate. Pour the remaining sauce over the chops and let them rest for 5 minutes before serving.

serving suggestion ✳ I like to serve these chops with white beans, Pesto-Parmesan Green Beans (page 243), or Garlic Cauliflower Mash (page 232).

Makes 4 servings ✳ **Total time:** about 20 minutes, plus 30 minutes marinating time
Per serving ✳ **Calories:** 350 ✳ **Protein:** 32g ✳ **Carbohydrates:** 3g ✳ **Fat:** 23g

Growing up, a dish my mom really loved was a classic blue cheese wedge salad, which meant I became a huge wedge salad lover. Something about the bacon with the crispy bed of iceberg lettuce always hit the spot for me.

The wedge salad from my childhood always had blue cheese dressing, but I change it up by using a creamy pesto-mayo dressing, which adds new flavor but still gives you a bit of the classic wedge taste. Iceberg lettuce is traditional because you can cut it in a nice wedge, but Little Gem lettuce would also work here. Feel free to include grilled chicken or steak with the salad for added protein.

blt wedge salad

Pesto-Mayo Dressing

¼ cup store-bought pesto

¼ cup light mayonnaise

¼ cup red wine vinegar

2 teaspoons hot honey

Kosher salt

Freshly ground
black pepper

Wedge Salad

1 head iceberg lettuce

1 pound center cut
bacon, cooked, then
crumbled (see Tip)

½ cup halved
cherry tomatoes

½ red onion, thinly sliced

1. Make the pesto-mayo dressing: In a small bowl, whisk together the pesto, mayonnaise, red wine vinegar, and hot honey until well combined. Add salt and pepper to taste.

2. Prepare the wedge salad: Remove any wilted outer leaves from the iceberg lettuce. Slice the head into quarters, cutting vertically toward the core, to create 4 large wedges. Then, cut the inner leaves of each wedge in a crosshatch pattern, cutting only about three-quarters of the way through to keep the wedge intact. If you'd like, you can remove a little of the cut-up lettuce to make more room for toppings.

3. To serve, place each wedge on a plate and top with crumbled bacon, tomatoes, and red onions. Pour the dressing generously over each wedge.

tip: I prefer center cut bacon because it has more protein than regular bacon, and I also think it has more flavor. You can cook the bacon however you'd like, but for a hands-off method, place it on a parchment-lined sheet pan and bake it at 400°F for 20 minutes, flipping once at the 15-minute mark. This method will give you bacon that is on the meatier side (as opposed to crispy).

Makes 4 servings ★ **Total time:** about 10 minutes
Per serving ★ **Calories:** 670 ★ **Protein:** 40g ★ **Carbohydrates:** 20g ★ **Fat:** 55g

Weekday meals can be so tricky. I love one-pot meals for this very reason. Everything cooks in a single dish in one go, leaving very little mess to clean up, and you don't have to worry about setting multiple timers, watching different pots on the stove, or checking the oven.

This low-carb, one-pot meal is inspired by Creole jambalaya, but I use cauliflower rice instead of white rice. The combination of andouille sausage, peppers, and onions simmered in Creole-seasoned tomatoes satisfies every time. I use Tony Chachere's Creole seasoning, but you can use any brand you like or make your own. Sautéed chicken or shrimp are also a nice addition to this dish, either alongside the sausage or in place of it.

sausage & cauliflower rice jambalaya

1 tablespoon salted butter

1 tablespoon extra-virgin olive oil

1 (12-ounce) package andouille sausage, sliced into ½-inch rounds

2 red bell peppers, finely diced

1 small yellow onion, finely diced

½ jalapeño, seeded and finely diced

2 garlic cloves, minced

2 (14-ounce) packages frozen cauliflower rice, thawed if frozen

1 (14.5-ounce) can diced tomatoes, drained

1 to 2 teaspoons Creole seasoning

1. Set a large pot over medium-high heat and add the butter and olive oil. Once the butter is melted and the pan is hot, add the sausage and sauté until browned, 4 to 5 minutes. Add the bell peppers and onion and continue to sauté until the vegetables are tender, about 5 minutes. Add the jalapeño and garlic and sauté until the garlic is fragrant, about 1 minute.

2. Add the cauliflower rice, tomatoes, and Creole seasoning. Continue to cook, stirring occasionally, until the cauliflower rice is tender and any liquid has cooked off, about 20 minutes. Serve hot.

Makes 4 servings * **Total time:** about 35 minutes
Per serving * **Calories:** 290 * **Protein:** 19g * **Carbohydrates:** 17g * **Fat:** 17g

sides

I make this simple cucumber salad multiple times a week—it is one of my absolute favorite recipes. I was inspired by a recipe for an Asian smashed cucumber salad, but I prefer the texture of extra-thinly sliced cucumber, so I use my mandolin (though you could also use a Y-shaped vegetable peeler to shave the cucumber into slices).

Once you try this recipe, I think it'll become a go-to for a quick weekday snack, a side dish for a family potluck, or a part of a weekend lunch spread. It's a high volume of vegetables, it pairs well with so many different proteins, it's super crunchy and refreshing, and it comes together in 5 minutes.

not-smashed cucumber salad

1 pound mini or regular cucumbers

2 tablespoons soy sauce

2 tablespoons seasoned rice vinegar

1 teaspoon garlic chili oil

1 teaspoon toasted sesame oil

1 teaspoon honey

Sesame seeds, for garnish

1. Thinly slice the cucumbers on a mandolin and place them in a medium mixing bowl.

2. To the same bowl, add the soy sauce, rice vinegar, garlic chili oil, sesame oil, and honey and toss until well combined. Garnish with sesame seeds and serve.

Makes 4 servings * **Total time:** about 5 minutes
Per serving * **Calories:** 50 * **Protein:** 2g * **Carbohydrates:** 7g * **Fat:** 3g

I'd like to thank the genius who figured out that cauliflower could be used in a mash instead of potatoes. Cauliflower isn't as starchy as potato, but its mild flavor and creamy texture when blended make it a perfect replacement—you won't even know the difference. I served this dish at a family dinner during the holidays, and my dad had no idea he was eating cauliflower. He was utterly shocked—and he's a Midwestern meat and potatoes sort of guy, so if he can be fooled, anyone can.

I feel like store-bought cauliflower mash always tastes watered down, and it's often full of unnecessary ingredients. This version is so flavorful, and you can have it ready in 20 minutes.

There are a couple of tricks to this recipe. First, don't skip boiling the garlic with the cauliflower—it's a simple step that adds a ton of flavor to the dish. Second, make sure to drain the cauliflower well and cook off any excess moisture before you blend it with the other ingredients. That will ensure you don't end up with a watery mash.

garlic cauliflower mash

1 head cauliflower, cut into large florets

3 garlic cloves, peeled but whole

2 tablespoons salted butter

¼ cup cream cheese

½ teaspoon garlic salt, plus more to taste

Freshly ground black pepper

1. Fill a large pot halfway with water and bring to a boil over high heat. Once boiling, add in the cauliflower florets and garlic cloves. Reduce the heat to medium and boil until the cauliflower is fork-tender, about 7 minutes. Drain the cauliflower and garlic cloves well using a colander. Remove the garlic cloves and set aside.

2. Return the drained cauliflower to the same pot. Set the pot over low heat and continue cooking. Use a wooden spoon to break up the cauliflower florets, allowing any remaining water to evaporate, about 5 minutes, or until the cauliflower begins sticking to the bottom of the pot.

3. In a food processor, combine the cauliflower, the reserved garlic cloves, butter, cream cheese, garlic salt, and black pepper to taste. Blend until the mixture is smooth and creamy, with no chunks remaining. Add more garlic salt to taste.

4. Transfer the cauliflower mash to a serving dish and enjoy hot.

serving suggestion ✳ Pair this with a juicy steak for the perfect meal that even my dad would love!

Makes 4 servings ✳ **Total time:** about 20 minutes
Per serving ✳ **Calories:** 140 ✳ **Protein:** 4g ✳ **Carbohydrates:** 9g ✳ **Fat:** 11g

This cabbage stir-fry is the perfect side dish to pair with Teriyaki Grilled Chicken (page 77)—it's actually based on my favorite combination at the mall food court. I like more heat, so I add sriracha, but you should season this to your own taste. You can use green or red cabbage (or a mixture of both for a colorful blend), but if you're short on time, pick up a bag of coleslaw mix at the grocery store to use instead. This side is perfect for meal prep—make a big batch and reheat as needed.

stir-fried cabbage

½ medium head cabbage, thinly sliced

2 tablespoons salted butter

3 garlic cloves, minced

1 tablespoon coconut aminos

1 teaspoon toasted sesame oil

½ tablespoon seasoned rice vinegar

½ teaspoon kosher salt

¼ teaspoon freshly ground black pepper

Sriracha to taste (optional)

1. Set a large skillet over medium-high heat. Add the cabbage and 2 tablespoons water. Cover with a lid and cook until the cabbage is tender, 4 to 5 minutes.

2. Move the cabbage to the side of the skillet and add the butter and garlic. Sauté until the butter is melted and the garlic is fragrant, about 1 minute. Stir to incorporate.

3. Add the coconut aminos, sesame oil, rice vinegar, salt, and pepper and toss to ensure the cabbage is evenly coated. Continue to sauté until the liquid reduces and the cabbage begins to caramelize, 5 to 7 minutes. Taste and adjust seasoning as desired. Serve hot with Sriracha, if desired.

Makes 4 servings ★ **Total time:** about 25 minutes
Per serving ★ **Calories:** 100 ★ **Protein:** 2g ★ **Carbohydrates:** 9g ★ **Fat:** 7g

Cauliflower rice isn't a one-for-one replacement for actual rice, but there are a lot of great things about it. It offers a neutral base that easily takes on the flavors of whatever seasonings you add—and you can give it so much flavor that you won't even miss regular rice. I think the key to this recipe is the chicken bouillon base, which adds a subtle richness that pairs well with most dishes.

garlic-herb cauliflower rice

1 (16-ounce) bag cauliflower rice, thawed if frozen

¼ cup chicken broth

1 teaspoon chicken bouillon (or 2 cubes)

2 garlic cloves, minced

1 tablespoon salted butter

¼ cup minced fresh parsley

1. Set a large skillet over medium-high heat. Add the cauliflower rice to the skillet, spreading it in an even layer. Cook, stirring occasionally, until most of the moisture has evaporated and the cauliflower begins to stick to the skillet, 5 to 7 minutes.

2. Pour the chicken broth into the skillet and stir to incorporate. Continue cooking until most of the chicken broth has been absorbed and the cauliflower rice is tender, 5 to 7 minutes.

3. Add the chicken bouillon, garlic, and butter. Stir until the butter is melted and the garlic is fragrant, 1 to 2 minutes. Fold in the parsley and serve hot.

tip: There are so many ways to change up this dish—this is just one variation. I love to add lime and cilantro to create cilantro-lime cauliflower rice, which I serve with taco bowls.

Makes 2 servings * **Total time:** about 20 minutes
Per serving * **Calories:** 120 * **Protein:** 6g * **Carbohydrates:** 13g * **Fat:** 6g

I always look forward to autumn because Brussels sprouts come into season. They're one of my all-time favorite vegetables, and you can technically find them year-round, but they're best in the fall. Brussels sprouts tend to be a bit bitter on their own, so I like to cook them with something sweet to balance them out, in this case, honey and balsamic.

The two-step roasting process in this recipe may seem complicated, but cooking them with the foil on at first allows them to steam in the oven, making them tender. Then, removing the foil and continuing to roast them gives them that nice caramelized exterior.

balsamic brussels sprouts

1 pound Brussels sprouts, trimmed and halved

1 tablespoon extra-virgin olive oil

1 teaspoon garlic salt

Freshly ground black pepper

2 teaspoons balsamic glaze

2 teaspoons honey

1. Preheat the oven to 425°F. Line a sheet pan with parchment paper or lightly grease it with olive oil.

2. In a large bowl, combine the Brussels sprouts with the olive oil, garlic salt, and black pepper to taste. Toss until evenly coated.

3. Spread the Brussels sprouts in a single layer on the prepared sheet pan. Cover the sheet pan tightly with foil and roast for 15 minutes.

4. After 15 minutes, remove the sheet pan from the oven. Remove the foil from the sheet pan and drizzle the balsamic glaze and honey over the Brussels sprouts. Toss to coat.

5. Return the sheet pan to the oven and continue to roast the Brussels sprouts until they are crispy and caramelized, 10 to 12 more minutes.

6. Transfer the Brussels sprouts to a serving dish and serve hot.

serving suggestion * You can serve these year-round, but they certainly make a classic holiday side dish. I love making them for Thanksgiving. Try adding crumbled bacon for extra savory richness.

Makes 4 servings * **Total time:** about 35 minutes
Per serving * **Calories:** 90 * **Protein:** 3g * **Carbohydrates:** 13g * **Fat:** 4g

To me, this is a classic recipe—I've been making these carrots for years. My dad asks for them at every holiday gathering. The way the honey caramelizes over the carrots is delicious. I like to use baby carrots for the ease of the dish, but you can also use regular carrots cut into bite-size pieces. Adjust the cooking time to your preference; I like them fork-tender.

honey butter–glazed carrots

1 quart chicken broth

1 pound baby carrots

2 tablespoons unsalted butter

3 tablespoons honey

¼ teaspoon dried thyme

Kosher salt

1. Set a medium pot over high heat. Add the chicken broth and bring to a boil.

2. Reduce the heat to medium and carefully add the carrots to the pot to avoid splashing yourself. Simmer the carrots until they are fork-tender, about 10 minutes.

3. Drain the carrots, then return them to the pot. (You can reserve the broth for another use; it'll be infused with sweet carrot flavor.) Set the pot over medium heat. Add the butter and let it melt.

4. Add the honey, thyme, and a few pinches of salt to the pot and cook, stirring frequently, until the mixture thickens to a glaze that coats the carrots, 8 to 10 minutes. Taste, and add more salt as desired.

5. Transfer the glazed carrots to a serving dish and enjoy hot.

serving suggestion * I tend to serve these carrots with prime rib, but they'd also be delicious with chicken thighs, salmon, or steak.

Makes 4 servings * **Total time:** about 25 minutes
Per serving * **Calories:** 150 * **Protein:** 2g * **Carbohydrates:** 26g * **Fat:** 6g

This is hands-down my favorite way to eat green beans. It's a staple recipe for me—just about the only way I ever cook them for myself.

I love the crisp snap of fresh green beans. There's no comparison; fresh is so much better than canned or frozen. I like to cook them until they're just tender so they're still bright green with a nice bite. This wonderfully easy side dish has minimal ingredients and uses staples I always keep on hand.

pesto–parmesan green beans

1 pound green beans, trimmed

1 cup chicken broth or water

2 tablespoons salted butter

3 garlic cloves, minced

Kosher salt

Freshly ground black pepper

1½ tablespoons store-bought pesto

2 tablespoons grated Parmesan cheese

1. In a large saucepan, combine the green beans and chicken broth. Bring to a boil over high heat. Reduce the heat to medium, cover, and simmer until the green beans are tender, about 5 minutes.

2. Drain the chicken broth out of the pot. (You can save the broth for another recipe; it will retain some of the green beans' flavor but is still usable!)

3. Add the butter to the pot with the green beans over medium heat, and allow the butter to melt. Add the garlic and cook, stirring frequently, until the garlic is fragrant and lightly golden, 1 to 2 minutes. Add salt and pepper to taste. Reduce the heat to low, stir in the pesto and Parmesan, and toss just until the Parmesan melts.

4. Serve hot.

serving suggestion ∗ These green beans work well with any protein, but I especially love them with Air-Fryer Pork Chops (page 221).

Makes 4 servings ∗ **Total time:** about 10 minutes
Per serving ∗ **Calories:** 120 ∗ **Protein:** 3g ∗ **Carbohydrates:** 9g ∗ **Fat:** 9g

Simple roasted broccoli is a great choice for a weekday side dish, but I make it so often that I started to get bored with the same basic flavor profiles: salt and pepper, lemon pepper, garlic salt, and so on. One day, wanting change things up, I added garlic chili oil, and suddenly this dish became a star! The flavors are so punchy, and if you add shrimp or chicken, you can even serve it as a complete meal. For more heat, add sriracha or your favorite hot sauce, but definitely don't skip the garlic chili oil—there are so many brands available in stores and online, and it's hard to find one that isn't delicious.

spicy roasted broccoli

1 large broccoli crown, cut into small florets

1 tablespoon extra-virgin olive oil

½ teaspoon garlic salt

Freshly ground black pepper

1 tablespoon salted butter, melted

1 tablespoon garlic chili oil

1. Preheat the oven to 425°F. Line a sheet pan with parchment paper or lightly grease it with olive oil.

2. In a large bowl, combine the broccoli, olive oil, garlic salt, and black pepper to taste and toss until evenly coated. Spread the broccoli in a single layer on the prepared sheet pan. Cover the pan with foil.

3. Roast for 10 minutes. Then remove the foil, return to the oven, and continue roasting until the broccoli begins to char, about 5 more minutes.

4. Meanwhile, in a small dish, whisk together the melted butter and garlic chili oil.

5. Pour the chili oil–butter mixture over the roasted broccoli and toss to coat. Serve hot.

serving suggestion *
This pairs really well with Mediterranean-Style Meatballs with Tzatziki Sauce (page 98), Air-Fryer Ginger-Garlic Ribs (page 205), or Egg Roll in a Bowl (page 202).

Makes 4 servings * **Total time:** about 20 minutes
Per serving * **Calories:** 210 * **Protein:** 6g * **Carbohydrates:** 5g * **Fat:** 19g

This is my homage to mac and cheese—I love to bring this to parties and family holiday gatherings. Cauliflower and cheese is such a classic, comforting dish, and it's also low-carb! The incredibly creamy cheese sauce is simple to make; no flour needed. I can't guarantee you'll have any leftovers, but if you do, just reheat the remaining servings in the oven so the cheese can return to a nice, bubbly golden brown.

cauliflower & cheese

1 large head cauliflower, cut into small bite-size florets

1 tablespoon salted butter

2 garlic cloves, minced

¾ cup heavy cream

1½ cups shredded sharp cheddar cheese

½ cup shredded mozzarella cheese

¼ cup grated Parmesan cheese

¼ teaspoon dry ground mustard

Kosher salt

Freshly ground black pepper

1. Preheat the oven to 425°F. Line a sheet pan with parchment paper.

2. Toss the cauliflower on the sheet pan. Roast it completely dry (no oil or seasoning) until the florets begin to char just slightly, 20 to 25 minutes.

3. Meanwhile, make the cheese sauce: In a small pot, melt the butter over medium-high heat. Add the garlic and sauté until fragrant, about 1 minute. Add the heavy cream and let the mixture simmer and thicken for about 3 minutes, stirring often to prevent scorching. Add in 1 cup of the cheddar cheese, all of the mozzarella and Parmesan, and the dry ground mustard and whisk to incorporate. Add salt and pepper to taste. Continue whisking until the cheese melts and the sauce is smooth.

4. Set the oven to broil.

5. Transfer the roasted cauliflower to a 9 by 13-inch baking dish, then pour the cheese sauce over the cauliflower and toss to coat. Top with the remaining ½ cup of cheddar cheese. Return to the oven and broil just until the cheese is bubbling and golden brown, about 3 minutes.

6. Serve hot.

serving suggestions ✻ This side pairs perfectly with grilled or roasted chicken or a rack of ribs.

Makes 8 servings ✻ **Total time:** about 35 minutes
Per serving ✻ **Calories:** 330 ✻ **Protein:** 15g ✻ **Carbohydrates:** 8g ✻ **Fat:** 27g

acknowledgments

Firstly, I want to thank God. I prayed for the career I have today and feel blessed to wake up every day and do what I truly love. I thank God for all the blessings in my life and never take a single opportunity for granted.

To Joe, my partner and most brutally honest recipe tester—thank you for being by my side through this entire journey. You are my biggest support, and your constant encouragement means so much.

To my mom, thank you for always being my most supportive and encouraging taste-tester. So many dishes you made for me growing up are part of the reason I love food and why I love cooking as much as I do today.

To my dad, thank you for being my first entrepreneurial role model. I learned what hard work looks like by watching you, and that work ethic has had a huge shape who I am today.

To Susan Roxborough, thank you for bringing me into the Clarkson Potter family.

To my editor, Francis Lam—thank you for being such a pleasure to work with. You helped turn this book into something I never could have imagined on my own, and your thoughtful guidance along the way has always been very appreciated.

To my literary agent, Amanda Bernardi, thank you for walking me through each step of this process with patience and care. Your encouragement and belief in this project from day one has meant the world to me.

To my writer, Erin, thank you for helping bring these headnotes to life. You took my ideas and stories and helped shape them into something that still feels like me—just more fun, more thoughtful, and more complete.

To my photographer, Matt, thank you for turning every recipe into something truly stunning. Your photos brought my book to life in ways I never dreamed possible.

To my food stylist, Adam, thank you for your precision and dedication to what you do. The care you put into every single dish made each recipe shine.

To the incredible design team at Clarkson Potter, thank you for taking my recipes and turning them into something so polished and beautiful. You truly made the book feel like me.

To my bestie Annie, you've been one of my biggest supporters from day one, and I'm so grateful for you on this ride!

And finally, to my followers, newsletter subscribers, and the incredible community that has supported me from the very beginning—this book is for you. Your support means everything to me, and I wouldn't be here without you.

index

Note: Page numbers in *italics* indicate recipe photos.

about the author

Jackie Hartlaub is a self-taught home cook and social media content creator (@lowcarbstateofmind). She launched her online platforms to share her journey following the keto diet. She has since shifted her focus toward high-protein content and shares realistic, easy recipes that make people want to cook their own food and grow confident in the kitchen.

CLARKSON POTTER/PUBLISHERS
An imprint of the Crown Publishing Group
A division of Penguin Random House LLC
1745 Broadway
New York, NY 10019
clarksonpotter.com
penguinrandomhouse.com

Library of Congress Cataloging-in-Publication Data
is available upon request

ISBN 978-0-593-80035-5
Ebook ISBN 978-0-59380036-2

Editor: Francis Lam
Editorial assistant: Darian Keels
Designer: Jan Derevjanik
Design manager: Mia Johnson
Art director: Stephanie Huntwork
Production editor: Serena Wang
Production manager: Jessica Heim
Production designer: Christina Self
Compositors: Merri Ann Morrell
  and Zoe Tokushige
Food and prop stylist: Adam Pearson
Photo and styling assistants: Wade Hammond
  and Diana Kim
Copyeditor: Allie Kiekhofer
Proofreaders: Christina Caruccio, Michelle Hubner,
  and Sasha Tropp
Indexer: Jay Kreider
Publicist: Natalie Yera-Campbell
Marketer: Andrea Portanova

Manufactured in China

10 9 8 7 6 5 4 3 2 1

First Edition

The authorized representative in the EU for product
safety and compliance is Penguin Random House
Ireland, Morrison Chambers, 32 Nassau Street, Dublin
D02 YH68, Ireland, https://eu-contact.penguin.ie.